"What the Otrembas offer in this incredible work is nothing less than a monumental paradigm shift for marriage enrichment experienced through the Divine Liturgy, every aspect of the liturgy, and Jesus embraced in the Most Holy Eucharist. To accept their offer is to have one's spiritual eyes wide open at every Mass, every marital encounter, and to be transformed into His beloved likeness."

—*Jim and Joy Pinto, Co-Hosts of EWTN's* At Home with Jim and Joy

"Their [the Otrembas'] practical suggestions, combined with solid Catholic teaching, help couples to realize the spiritual connection between the Mass and their marriage. You'll never attend Mass again without thinking of how it does impact and strengthen your marriage."

—*Veola Burchett, Director, Family and Pro-life Office*
Catholic Diocese of Salt Lake City, UT

"Using their gifts and personal journey, they skillfully and prayerfully tied the sacramentality of marriage to the Eucharist. Every married couple could benefit from this practical, skills-based material; no matter if you are newlyweds or married 45 plus years."

—*Deacon Tom Lang, Director, Office of the Permanent Diaconate*
Archdiocese of Dubuque, IA

"Best workshop I have been to."

—*Deacon participant, married 50 years*

"In only 7 hours, you have helped us a thousand times more than the four marriage counseling meetings we went to! Your presence here today is a gift from God. I deeply thank you for giving us tools to strengthen and improve our marriage. I have prayed for help and I know that you are part of His answer."

—*Participant, married 5 years*

Banquet of Love: The Eucharist as Weekly Marriage Enrichment
A Workbook to Transform Your Marriage Through the Power of the Eucharist

Copyright © 2019, Grace and Truth Resources, LLC

Nihil obstat: Rev. Robert C. Harren, J.C.L., Censor deputatus
Imprimatur: Most Rev. Donald J. Kettler, D.D., Bishop of St. Cloud, October 14, 2016

Printed and Manufactured in the United States of America
1 2 3 4 5 6 7 8 9 10

Contents

i

Why Eucharist as Weekly Marriage Enrichment?

It is a scene we recreate every time we participate in the Eucharist, but on most occasions the intimacy of the moment is lost on us. So let's return for a moment to the first Eucharist and recapture the intimacy of that moment our Lord shared with His disciples.

There He was, the homeless teacher, surrounded by His rag-tag band of followers. For the previous three years, they had lived with Him and followed Him from Galilee to Jerusalem. They had seen Him cure crippling diseases, raise the dead to life, encounter the religious authorities and best them in matters of the law, and challenge His listeners with stories of camels and needles, prodigal fathers and wayward sons, tax collectors, and righteous Samaritans. They had marveled as He somehow made enough out of five loaves and two small fish to feed thousands. Now in Jerusalem, the great City of Peace, the place where He had predicted His own death, they gathered one last time to share the meal so steeped in spiritual and historical significance that it meant the world to their people.

"With great longing have I desired to share this Passover meal with you," He told his friends, knowing that this would be the final meal of His earthy life.

And so, to make an everlasting remembrance of that time and place, the man whose followers called Him Rabbi, "Teacher," the devout Jew who had come not to abolish the Law but to fulfill it, deviated from the centuries-old formula of the Jewish Passover meal to institute a new covenant, a new promise between heaven and earth, a never-before experienced means for His followers to remember Him, to partake of Him, to share Him with generations yet unborn. He gave them His body and blood under the forms of earthly bread and wine, His very self under cover of table food and drink.

The intimacy of that moment is indescribable. The Lord of Life chose to make Himself known to us through the common elements of our lives: bread and wine, water and oil, touch, fire, and words. And yet, that very "stooping" to our human level can make the enormity of the thing practically imperceptible. We take for granted that God is here in this bread and wine, and is among us in the gathered community.

We need to step back and consider a prayer common among the Orthodox Christians as they receive Eucharist: "I hold You who hold the world; I take You who govern the universe, and I am about to put You into my mouth."

Christian marriage embodies a similar intimacy—the fusing of two lives in their hopes and dreams, their daily work and play, their very flesh to create a new entity capable of imparting life. And, just as the intimacy of the Eucharist is easily lost on us because the elements are so "common," because the intimacy of Christian marriage is the very stuff of life, the activities that humankind is engaged in each and every day, the vital truth of the intimacy it involves can escape us.

To be fair, we cannot operate on a daily basis with an acute awareness of the mystery that surrounds us. That would be like living at the crest of a roller coaster on the very brink of taking the exhilarating plunge down a 100-foot drop! We can't sustain that kind of high alert. But it does help to admit that we live with factors that desensitize us to the mystery.

The intent of this workbook is to invite married Catholic couples to explore the mystery of their shared life in Christ, who gave Himself for us so that we might live. Christian marriage has as its premise the belief that spouses enter into this union in order to realize and fully live their baptismal call, the life they share in Christ by virtue of their baptism.

For Catholics, the centerpiece of this life in Christ is the great mystery of the Eucharist, in which we are fed by Christ Himself. But the Eucharist is more than mere nourishment; it is a true pattern for our lives.

Overview of the Workbook

In this workbook, we examine the entire Eucharistic liturgy as a model for married life. Each part of the liturgy informs our sacramental life together, from gathering to penitence, from breaking open the Word to partaking of the very Body and Blood of Christ.

Each act and rite of the Eucharist provides a different form of intimacy that holds promise for our growth as husband and wife, members of the Body of Christ.

Each section of this workbook ends with suggested activities for reflection, prayer, and action. Our hope is that these activities will serve to revitalize Catholic marriages. By taking time to examine the different elements of intimacy in the

Eucharist and the factors that obscure its power for us, we open ourselves to the working of the Holy Spirit in our lives and in our marriages.

A special and central feature of this workbook is what we call the "foundational intimacies": eight modes of being present to and with each other in marriage that flow from the Eucharistic liturgy.

These are the eight foundational intimacies:

- **Spiritual**. Praying together, going to Church together, reading the Bible or devotional together, etc. We believe this to be the most important one because we are made in the image and likeness of God. Sometimes our experiences in the physical world can work against us and we forget that we have a spiritual soul created directly by God.

- **Verbal**. Talking and listening and reassuring each other they are loved, respecting each other privately and personally, etc.

- **Emotional**. Validating feelings, sharing feelings, creating feelings of security, processing feelings, etc.

- **Intellectual**. Sharing ideas, honoring each other, understanding differences between intimacy and sex, understanding different needs for males and females, forgiving each other, etc.

- **Temporal**. Hanging out together as a couple and family with no agenda and no electronics, working out together, doing hobbies together, etc.

- **Family**. Sharing family time together with no electronics, sharing meal time with no electronics, working together, etc.

- **Physical**. Physical appearance, hand holding, kissing. This is *not* sexual intimacy.

- **Intimacy of absence**. Christ taught us about this during His ascension into Heaven. This form of intimacy points to the need for proactive and productive separate time alone in marriage. This is a tricky one and needs to be understood and acted on, and is not recommended for couples with long absences from each other in the military, opposite work shifts, etc.

How to Use this Workbook

There is no "one-way" to use this workbook. It can be used at the personal level (working through it as a married couple for 20 minutes a day) or at the parish or diocesan level. The key is to use the material in a way that best suits your schedule and situation. That said, we offer a few recommendations.

For Personal Use:

- Commit to devoting at least 20 minutes a day to using this text as a personal devotional workbook at home. It doesn't take much time, but it does take consistent and correct applications that the Church offers every time She celebrates the Eucharist, which is the best model for our marriages!

For Use in a Parish:

- The parish can form a Eucharistic Marriage Group that meets each week for seven or eight weeks until the material is covered. At the beginning of each meeting the facilitator can "check in" with the couples to see how they have been using the material they studied during the previous week. To "train" the facilitators, the parish can provide them with a copy of this workbook to go through ahead of time to ensure that they understand the material and how best to utilize it in the group. This is a great model because it offers time to assimilate the information between sessions, which can lead to practicing the behaviors necessary for a healthy, holy marriage.

- The parish can host a Eucharistic Marriage Retreat on a Saturday from 9 a.m. to 4 p.m., offer the Sacrament of Reconciliation at 4 p.m., and close with Mass at 5 p.m. This day retreat would be led by facilitators who have mastered the material in the workbook and know how best to present it to retreating couples. This is a great model because many couples who are not willing to commit to seven or eight weeks will participate in a one-day retreat. The authors love to come to parishes and train facilitators or use Skype or other types of interactive technology to train. Email Jim for more information: jimotremba@gmail.com.

Glossary

Before we begin our practical Eucharistic theology, let's define some key terms, as some may be unfamiliar or need clarification. Here is a list of the words you see in this workbook:

- **"Anamnesis"** is a Greek word that means "to recall or to remember." Theologically, however, this is not a simple remembering the way a calendar "remembers" what date it is. Instead, through the Holy Spirit, in every Eucharist we participate in the life, death, and resurrection of Christ our Lord! Moreover, we also participate in Christ's sending us the love between Him and Abba: the Holy Spirit.

- **"Assembly"** means the people gathered for public prayer. Before Vatican II (1962–1965) a priest could celebrate Mass alone, and the rite for Mass didn't involve the assembly at all. After Vatican II, the assembly has played a critical part in the Mass.

- **"CCC"** is the *Catechism of the Catholic Church*, published in 1993.

- **"Dei Verbum"** is a Latin phrase that means "The Word of God." This is one of two "Dogmatic Constitutions" from Vatican II. Dei Verbum's main theme is divine revelation.

- **"Consecrated"** means to be "set apart" or "made holy." The priest consecrates the bread and wine at Mass and they become the real body and blood of Christ, even though they still look, feel, and taste like bread and wine. All baptized Christians are consecrated to God as holy.

- **"Doxology"** is a Greek word meaning "glory," and we give God glory all the time, but especially toward the end of the Eucharistic Prayer, when we pray "Through Him, with Him, in Him. . . ."

- **"Epiclesis"** is a Greek word that refers to the time during the Liturgy of the Eucharist (the second half of the Mass) when the Holy Spirit is called to come down upon the gifts of bread and wine and transform them into the Body and Blood of Christ. It also refers to the calling down of the Holy Spirit on the assembly in order to change us into the Body of Christ.

- **"Eucharist"** is a Greek word that means "thanksgiving."

- **"Four Major Parts of Each Mass"**: (1) Introductory Rites, (2) Liturgy of the Word, (3) Liturgy of the Eucharist, and (4) Concluding Rites.

- **"Incarnation"** means God's becoming a human in Jesus, which we celebrate at Christmas.

- **"Institution Narrative"** are the words from the Gospels of Matthew, Mark, and Luke that contain the words of consecration in the presider's prayers ("this is my Body . . . this is my Blood"). The Gospel of John has no institution narrative, but rather a lengthy discussion of the Bread of Life (Chapter 6).

- **"Intimacy"** is a word we use in the strictest sense of the literal meaning of the word, that is: "inner-most." We talk about many kinds of intimacy (verbal, emotional, temporal, etc.).

- **"Liturgy"** is a Greek word meaning "work of the people" or "public work." We use the word now to describe a public, official prayer of the Catholic Church: the Liturgy of the Hours (official prayer of the Catholic Church) or the Liturgy (meaning the Mass).

- **"Lumen Gentium"** is a Latin phrase that means "light to the nations." It is one of two "Dogmatic Constitutions" from Vatican II, promulgated by Pope Paul VI on November 21, 1964. Lumen Gentium's main theme is evangelization and a universal call to holiness; in other words, the laity are called to holiness and to bring their holiness to the "marketplace."

- **"Oblation"** is a Latin word that means "offering." In the Eucharist the Holy Spirit works through the priest and the assembly to offer up to God that which He has freely given to us: His only Son, Christ our Lord.

- **"Paradox"** means two things that cannot logically go together. An example would be a "square circle."

- **"Paten"** is a small silver or gold plate that is used to hold the hosts for Mass.

- **"Rite"** means a specific part of the Catholic Mass (or Eucharist).
For example, in the Gathering Rite, we gather to begin the celebration of the Mass.

- **"Transubstantiation"** is a scholarly term adopted in the Middle Ages to define what happens to the bread and wine when they are consecrated at every Eucharist. They are transformed into the real Body, Blood, Soul, and Divinity of Christ even though they continue to look like bread and wine.

- **"Triduum"** means "three days." The Sacred Triduum begins on the evening of Holy Thursday and concludes on the evening of Easter Sunday.

Practical Eucharistic Theology

1

Hundreds of graduate courses are taught on Eucharistic theology, and throughout the centuries, tens of thousands of pages have been written on the subject. Because we cannot possibly go into the detail that this subject deserves in our little workbook, we admit at the outset that this section has some significant limitations. To better understand how our marriages are Eucharistic, however, we first need a better understanding of Eucharistic theology.

The Sacredness of a Meal

For the Jewish person in Christ's time, a meal was sacred: there was no division between sacred and secular. A meal was intimate and sacred. Something (animal or plant) has to give its life for us to eat, and this is sacred and intimate. This speaks a profound truth that the Eucharist is meant for: **sacrificial love for new life**. Our marriages must mirror this same truth in order to be all that the Lord wants for our marriages: an icon of God's faithful love for all of humanity in order to bring about new life, in many different forms.

Jesus would have been steeped in this understanding of the inherent sacredness of a meal. As a Jewish rabbi, He would have taught it as a matter of course. Sharing a meal is intimate and sacred: that is the air Jesus breathed. We lose sight of this in our 21st century American society as we drive through a fast food joint and wolf down a burger on the go. We forget the inherent intimacy and sacrificial nature of a meal.

Because the Jews considered a meal holy and sacrificial, many Jewish celebrations were configured around a meal. A primary example is the Passover.

The Passover celebrated how God freed the ancient Israelites from Egyptian slavery, detailed in Exodus, chapter 12. The Passover is that night when the Israelites were protected from death because the blood from an unblemished male lamb was applied to the entrances of the Israelites homes. The Israelites were commanded to eat the flesh of that sacrificed lamb and share this sacred meal in community. Death "passed over" those houses that were marked with the blood of the lamb whose flesh had been consumed.

When the Jews of Jesus' time (i.e. 2000 years ago) celebrated the Passover, they weren't merely remembering a historical event (being freed from Egyptian slavery). Rather, they believed God's love for them was so powerful that the reality of the past was made present to them, and they were able to participate in the freedom of the historical Passover. The past was made present!

When Jesus celebrated the Passover with his disciples, He fulfilled this celebration as He gave to us the first Eucharist. He is the Lamb of God, whose sacrifice frees us from eternal death and separation from God. At the Last Supper He instructed His disciples to eat His flesh and drink His blood. The Eucharist is now the unbloody perpetual sacrifice that we can celebrate every day (except Good Friday).

When we celebrate the Eucharist, we truly believe that Christ is really present: body, blood, soul, and divinity. Jesus nourishes us to become more of who we are as members of the Body of Christ, and become truly present and attentive to each other. Just like the Jewish community during the time of Jesus, we believe that when we celebrate the Eucharist, the past is made present, and we participate in the perfect sacrifice of Jesus to God the Father (through the life, death, and resurrection of Jesus, and sending of the Holy Spirit). We participate in this Paschal Mystery every time the Eucharist is celebrated.

Every Eucharist moves us from sin to salvation through the sacrifice of Jesus Christ, the Lamb of God who takes away the sins of the world and reconciles us back to the Father through His Holy Spirit.

The Eucharist Must Lead to Loving Service

The Gospel of John (written around 100 A.D.) is unique because it does not have the Institution Narrative (i.e., Jesus' instituting the Sacrament of the Eucharist at the Last Supper). Instead, in the Gospel of John we read about Jesus' washing of His disciples' feet, showing us that Eucharist must lead to loving service. Here we have the Lord of life, who was with the Father before all ages, taking the place of a slave. **If we are to follow our Master, we need to make sure that every Eucharist we celebrate leads to service of our neighbor.**

The Eucharist and Marriage are Both Unitive and Procreative in Nature

Because the Eucharist celebrates Jesus' eternal sacrifice to the Father, it is both unitive and procreative. It is unitive because as we partake of the Eucharist, we become one in the Body of Christ. Furthermore, the Eucharist is procreative because it begets new life within us through the Paschal Mystery. Our share in the life, death, and resurrection of Jesus Christ solidifies our identity as adopted sons and daughters of God.

Like the Eucharist, marriage possesses both a unitive and a procreative nature. Marriage is unitive in that it makes the couple one flesh. Marriage is procreative in that it brings about new life through physical, emotional, and spiritual progeny. This is the very nature of marriage.

So, every Eucharist we celebrate brings about new life and intimately unites us together as the one Body of Christ.

Vatican II Affirms This Intimate Union at Every Eucharist

Theology of Vatican II (1962 - 1965) affirms that every Eucharist is an intimate union with Christ and one another (CCC 1391).

Therefore, we boldly profess that Christ is not only on the altar, but around the altar: the living Body of Christ in the assembly. Moreover, with the advent of Vatican II, the Eucharist is a way to strengthen our love (CCC 1394) as well as to increase our baptismal life (CCC 1392). This call to Eucharistic intimate love and increased baptismal life is now our invitation and challenge in each marriage. Now, we'll move into the "blueprint" of every Eucharist.

The Blueprint of Every Eucharist

Every Eucharist mirrors life in that it has a specific order and flow to it. In our life (we are both part-time stay-at-home parents), we find it much easier to fully participate in life when we understand what is coming next, through communicating and understanding our schedules.

In the Eucharist, it is easier to actively, consciously, and fully participate when we take time to understand what is "coming next" through the Order of the Mass.

Every Mass has four major themes or "parts": (1) Introductory Rites, (2) Liturgy of the Word, (3) Liturgy of the Eucharist, and (4) Concluding Rites.

The First Part of Each Mass Begins With the "Introductory Rites"

- The Entrance Procession (usually a song while the presider enters the church and kisses the altar).
- The Liturgical Greeting (all make the Sign of the Cross).
- The Penitential Act (in which we ask God for mercy). This is usually different during the Easter Season when we sometimes have the blessing of water and the Sprinkling Rite.

- Gloria (this ancient song is used on all Sundays except in Advent and Lent).
- Collect (this is a prayer that is said by the presider and all answer "Amen").

The Second Part of the Mass is "The Liturgy of the Word"

- First Reading (each Mass has a different first reading).
- Responsorial Psalm (usually a sung response from the Psalms).
- Second Reading (we use the second reading for all Sundays and solemnities).
- Gospel Acclamation (usually a sung "Alleluia," except during Lent when we do not use the "Alleluia" in our liturgies).
- Gospel (each Mass has a different Gospel selection).
- Homily (ideally each Homily acts as a "bridge" from the Liturgy of the Word to the Liturgy of the Eucharist—all based on the readings of the day).
- The Profession of Faith (on Sundays and solemnities).
- Universal Prayers (prayers of the faithful).

The Third Part of the Mass is "The Liturgy of the Eucharist"

- Presentation of the Gifts and Preparation of the Altar.
- Prayer over the Gifts.
- Eucharistic Prayer.
- The Lord's Prayer.
- Sign of Peace.
- Lamb of God.
- Communion Rite.
- Prayer after Communion.

The Fourth Part of the Mass is "The Concluding Rites"

- Announcements, if needed.
- Greeting and Blessing.
- Dismissal (we are told to go and proclaim the Gospel with our lives).

Reflection Questions on Practical Eucharistic Theology

Answer the questions individually first and then share your responses with your spouse:

1. What is your understanding of the Eucharist? How has this section affirmed or challenged that understanding?

_____

_____

_____

_____

_____

2. How does the Catholic doctrine of Christ being around the altar affect your celebration of the Eucharist?

_____

_____

_____

_____

_____

3. What are some of the factors that make it difficult for you to recognize the intimacy of the Eucharist when you participate in Mass?

_____

_____

_____

_____

_____

4. The Eucharist is now seen as a way to "strengthen our baptismal life." What is something that you can do this week to strengthen your own or your spouse's baptismal life?

_____

_____

_____

_____

_____

5. Did you gain any insights from the "blueprint of every Eucharist"? If so, how can they help you fully celebrate at the next Eucharist you attend?

_____

_____

_____

_____

_____

Notes

The Introductory Rites (Gathering Rites)   2

Although the Gathering Rite officially starts when the presider begins to process into the Church, Jim and Maureen love to have a "domestic (at-home) gathering" in their van on the way to Mass. They thank God for Jesus and the Holy Spirit, and they take turns asking their children who they want to pray for during the sacred Mass. This practice helps them prepare for the liturgy.

The Gathering Rite is full of different forms of intimacy, including:

* **Emotional intimacy** (we usually gather with a song)

* **Physical intimacy** (we sometimes greet each other with a handshake or hug)

The Power of Music

When we arrive at church and the liturgical Introductory Rites begin, it is good to think about the words of Beethoven: "Music can change the world!"

We certainly know it can change the liturgy (for good or ill). It is with great joy and exultation that we begin each liturgy with an uplifting song of praise (unless it is a daily Mass, Advent, or Lent).

The Church knows the power of music and uses it beautifully. Music is used throughout the entire liturgy, and it is ideal to begin every Eucharistic celebration with a song of praise.

We may not think about it, but the Introductory Rites are filled with several intimacies, including emotional intimacy (we feel welcomed), family intimacy (we gather as adopted sons of daughters of God . . . one family), spiritual intimacy (we gather to worship the King of Kings), and verbal intimacy.

Devote some time now to the following questions about the Gathering Rite at your parish (answer individually first and then share your responses with your spouse):

1. Is music valued in your parish?

_____

_____

_____

_____

2. Do you participate with the voice God gave you?

_____

_____

_____

_____

_____

It is good to pause and reflect on the role that music plays in our marriages. Music in general has the power to lift up or tear down, and the words of the songs can create within us habits of virtue or vice.

The songs we listen to throughout the day are what we unconsciously think about, and they slowly shape our thoughts, mood, and actions. We need to allow the Holy Spirit to challenge us so that the music we listen to will help our life and marriage.

The power of the Lord, given to us through the Eucharist, is what gives us strength to face the times when our marriage is in a minor key.

Reflection Questions on Music

Answer the questions individually first and then share your responses with your spouse:

1. What are the songs that you have memorized? Take a few minutes to list some of the top 20 songs that you know by heart.

_____

_____

_____

_____

_____

2. This list of songs is impacting you at an unconscious level, whether you know it or not. These are your "go-to" songs. Do these songs build you and your marriage up or tear you down?

_____

_____

_____

_____

_____

3. How might Jesus respond to the lyrics of these songs?

_____

_____

_____

_____

_____

4. Is the Holy Spirit asking you to examine your choice of music in your life?

_____

_____

_____

_____

_____

5. Do you ever listen to Christian music?

_____

_____

_____

_____

_____

The Sign of the Cross

After the opening song, the presider invites us all to make the Sign of the Cross. Some do so very sloppily, others very reflectively and reverently. But what does the Sign of the Cross have to do with our marriage? Absolutely everything!

The only reason we had the power and privilege to confer the Sacrament of Marriage upon each other is because of our baptism. We make the Sign of the Cross to remind ourselves of our great identity through baptism. By baptism we are made members of the Body of Christ, and it is only because we are baptized and confirmed (both sacraments of initiation) that we can participate fully in the intimacy of the Eucharist.

All of this, and much more, lies in the "tiny," often unnoticed, symbol of the Sign of the Cross. Here are some connections between the Sign of the Cross and the Sacrament of Marriage:

As we make the Sign of the Cross we name our God a Triune God: Father, Son, and Holy Spirit. Our God has always been, and will ever remain, in relationship as a Trinity, and the Trinity will ever be in relationship with the Body of Christ, both in heaven and on earth. We share in that divine life of the Trinity through our baptism!

When we make the Sign of the Cross we remind ourselves that we are created **from** relationship (with God and our parents) and that we are created **for** relationship (in our vocation of marriage). By our baptism we share in Christ's one priesthood. When Jim and Maureen present workshops, they sometimes like to ask how many priests are in the assembly. Only every now and then will a brave lay person raise his or her hand, at which point we give a cheer!

All of the baptized share in the One Priesthood of Jesus Christ. We so boldly read this in the Scriptures:

> "Come as living stones, and let yourselves be used in building the spiritual temple, where you will serve as holy priests to offer spiritual and acceptable sacrifices to God through Jesus Christ" (1 Peter 2:5).

Our Catholic theology makes a distinction between the priesthood of the laity (called the "ordinary priesthood") and the ministerial priesthood of the ordained priest or bishop.

We all share in the One Priesthood of Christ. Because we are priests in our marriage, we need to ask, "What is the role of a priest?" The primary role of a priest, as we just read in 1 Peter, chapter 2, is to offer sacrifice and to unite all our sacrifices to the one sacrifice of Christ through His cross and resurrection.

Each marriage and family has many sacrifices to "offer" up to the Lord on a daily basis. It could be the stress of caring for an ill spouse or family member, the hurts we hear as parish ministers, the "mundane" tasks of paying bills, cleaning kitchens, or helping our grandchildren learn how to read. When we think about it, our marriages and families have much to lift up as a lived prayer to Abba, and when we do this on a regular basis, we help build up the Body of Christ.

Because we are priests, we can bless our spouses. We bless ourselves with the holy water every time we start the Mass. Are we intentional about having holy water at home?

1. How does the idea of blessing your spouse appeal to you?

_____

_____

_____

_____

_____

2. When would be good time to exchange a blessing with your spouse? (e.g. upon waking; before going to sleep)

_____

_____

_____

_____

3. If you have been given the gift of children, when is the last time you blessed your children?

_____

_____

_____

_____

_____

We can exercise our domestic priesthood by blessing our spouse and loved ones. The blessing of our children is contained in the baptismal rite, and for some parents that is the last time they bless their children. Jim and Maureen's hope is that you have been blessing your children regularly (because you share in Christ's Priesthood), or that you will now consider this invitation to do so.

If this idea of blessing your spouse or your children or grandchildren is new to you, here is a new ritual you can do based on the Gathering Rite of the Mass: When you hug each other before you leave for the day, the husband can make a cross on the forehead of his wife and say: "God bless your day, honey, in the name of the Father, and of the Son, and of the Holy Spirit." Then the wife can do the exact same blessing for her husband. These rituals help us to nurture our marriage and strengthen it while bringing to new life the same ritual we do at every Eucharist: the Sign of the Cross.

So the Sign of the Cross reminds us that we are all connected to Christ, the Church, and each other through our common baptism. But when we make the Sign of the Cross we actually trace a cross on our body. Why is that?

We make a cross because all relationships this side of heaven will bring a measure of darkness, sacrifice, and suffering from the fall of humanity ("original sin").

Marriage is difficult work—very worth it, but difficult work. But all of those suffering moments have been redeemed by what we celebrate at every Eucharist: the paschal mystery, also known as the life, death, and resurrection of Jesus and the sending of the Holy Spirit into our lives.

The Sign of the Cross can remind us of all these truths if we take time to think and pray about it.

Three Additional Applications for the Sign of the Cross

1. It is a helpful practice to have holy water at home and bless each other with that holy water. If you are not doing so, we invite you to begin doing so today. The Catholic Church calls holy water "sacramental" because it reminds us of the Sacrament of Baptism if we take time to ponder it.

2. During your shower or bath, the water can remind you of your own baptism. When you are in the shower or bath you can say a little prayer such as, "Lord, may I remain faithful to my baptismal identity: I am Your child, I am a priest, prophet, and king (or queen). Help me today to know You are with me."

3. In the morning when you wake up, put your hand on your heart and remind yourself of your identity as a son or daughter of God. Here is the prayer we recommend:

> *For women:* "God, thank you for adopting me and making me your
> daughter. I am good enough just as I am. You love me so much.
> Help me to be the best daughter I can be today. Amen."

> *For men:* Put your hand on your heart and say "God, thank you for adopting
> me and making me your son. Help me to be the leader you want me to
> be through loving service. You have great plans for me and you
> love me so much. Help me to be the best son I can be today. Amen."

Follow this prayer by making the Sign of the Cross on your heart or over your heart.

4. After reading and processing the information on the Sign of the Cross, write down some other major points that you learned and want to remember:

_____

_____

_____

_____

_____

5. Write down two specific attitudes and actions that you will do today with your spouse to live out the beauty of the Sign of the Cross in your Sacrament of Marriage:

_____

_____

_____

_____

_____

Predictability and Possibility in the Eucharistic Liturgy

Every Eucharistic Liturgy is structured with predictability and pregnant with possibility.

Liturgy is, by its nature, predictable. In other words, it follows a set pattern, and the congregation has a good idea of what to expect, when to sit and stand, etc. This predictability can be comforting but can also lead to unexamined routine ("going through the motions").

Likewise, there are both positives and negatives to possibility as well. The greatest possibility is what the Holy Spirit can do in our lives, our parishes, and our marriages. Since the Eucharist is "the source and summit of the Christian life" (*Lumen Gentium*, no. 11), there is unlimited possibility for growth and new life at the celebration of each Mass.

But, in our brokenness, there can also be a negative side to possibility, which can distract us from prayerfully entering into the ritual flow of the liturgy. For example, think about the last time you were at a Mass with too many surprises (e.g. too many unfamiliar hymns) and how jarring it was to the majority of the assembly. What we need is balance between the predictability and possibility inherent in the Eucharistic Liturgy. But this requires direct attention to, and reflection on, the healthy tension that exists between Eucharistic predictability and Eucharistic possibility. Let's take time now to reflect upon these.

Reflection Questions on Eucharistic Predictability and Possibility

Answer the questions individually first and then share your responses with your spouse:

1. Think about the last Eucharist that you celebrated. What were some predictable elements?

_____

_____

_____

_____

_____

2. Would you describe these as negative or positive? Why?

_____

_____

_____

_____

_____

3. Think about the last Eucharist that you celebrated. Name some "possibilities" (i.e. features that were new or different).

_____

_____

_____

_____

_____

4. Would you describe these as positive or negative? Why?

_____

_____

_____

_____

_____

5. Think about the next Eucharist you will celebrate. How will thinking and praying about a healthy tension between Eucharistic predictability and possibility help you to more fully and consciously participate?

_____

_____

_____

_____

_____

Connections to Your Marriage: Predictability and Possibility

Each marriage contains dynamics similar to the Eucharistic Gathering Rite. Every marriage has positive and negative elements of predictability and possibility.

As a licensed therapist, Jim has worked with many couples whose marriages have a negative predictable dynamic of using tones and volumes during communication that build barriers instead of bridges. Tone and volume in communication can become a negative predictable pattern that God desires to heal.

There can also be many positive predicable elements in a marriage. In our marriage, for example, Maureen knows that Jim will routinely call before coming home from work to see if she needs anything and to communicate with her. That is positive predictability. Jim knows that Maureen will pay their bills on time and will have most of the meals prepared. Maureen knows that Jim will have the kitchen clean most of the time. These are all positive predictabilities in our marriage.

What about your marriage? Devote some time now to answer the reflection questions.

Reflection Questions on Marital Predictability and Possibility

Answer the questions individually first and then share your responses with your spouse:

1. In the Gathering Rite we recall that Christ re-creates us every day in God's image and likeness. There is great predictability in that truth. Identify three positive actions or attitudes that are predictable in your marriage or spouse. For example, "I can count on my spouse to take out the trash without asking."

_____

_____

_____

_____

_____

2. Sometimes predictability can take on negative dimensions, and God's possibility for our marriage can be obscured, creating marital stagnation. Are there areas in your marriage where this is true? For example, "Every time I bring up a difficult subject my spouse clams up."

_____

_____

_____

_____

_____

3. Given what you identified in the previous question, how can you invite God to bring life-giving possibility into those situations?

_____

_____

_____

_____

_____

4. What are some insights from this chapter that you will apply to your marriage?

_____

_____

_____

_____

_____

The Penitential Act

3

As the Introductory Rite continues, we are invited to recognize that we have a loving God who desires to forgive us. God lives for giving. The Penitential Act is structured with different types of intimacy. They include:

- **Intellectual intimacy** (we think about the areas that we need to ask for mercy)

- **Spiritual intimacy** (we trust in God's love)

- **Verbal intimacy** (we speak words that seek mercy)

God desires to give us forgiveness and always invites us to ask for mercy, but especially during the Penitential Act. When God forgives, God redeems. God desires to forgive our sins and then turn those sins and hurts into new life.

Connections to Your Marriage: The Penitential Act

This "passover" from sin to salvation is at the heart of the Eucharist. Jesus desires to take our sins and hurts and create new life from them. This can't happen if we don't let go of our sins and regrets and give them to the Lord during the Penitential Act.

When we let go of them, a miracle will happen. Slowly, we learn to leave our regrets behind us and focus on how only the Holy Spirit transforms regret into reconciliation—with God, ourselves, and each other.

In the early Church, the Eucharist was the primary celebration of forgiveness and reconciliation. That is why the Penitential Act is included at the beginning of the Liturgy.

This does not minimize the role of the Sacrament of Reconciliation but rather elevates the Eucharist to a fuller understanding of what it means to be the source and summit of our faith.

It helps if we understand that the Lord desires a "domestic" (at home) penitential act as well.

We are firm believers that if married couples follow the wisdom of the Eucharist and create a domestic penitential act in their marital relationships, divorce rates will plummet!

We can recognize and replicate this ancient practice every day in our marriage and family. And the sooner we begin, the quicker we will realize what psychology has taught us for almost three decades: When I forgive somebody who hurts me, it helps *me* by lowering my blood pressure and bringing more balance into my life.

Following are 12 building blocks to construct a domestic penitential act in our marriages and families. Note that these "blocks" apply to hurts within the marital relationship as well as hurts that either spouse has experienced outside of the marriage (e.g., family of origin, workplace, etc.).

12 Building Blocks to Construct a Domestic Penitential Act

1st Block: The Sacrament of Reconciliation

As Catholics we have the powerful Sacrament of Reconciliation for forgiveness, and we need to use it frequently. The wisdom of Padre Pio, the 20th-century stigmatist, summed it up well: even clean rooms need frequent dusting. Yes, we need cleaning and dusting. Yet, even after we have been forgiven in this sacrament, we can still feel the need to process that forgiveness. Recall the story of Peter's denial of Jesus. Peter was forgiven, but he needed to process those feelings of shame, hurt, regret, etc., with someone he trusted (see John chapter 21 for the story of Jesus and Peter on the seashore after the Resurrection). We need to do the same: We need to have safe people in our lives with whom we can process our feelings.

2nd Block: Forgiveness is a Paradox

Forgiveness is tricky. It is both a decision and a process. It is a decision because it involves using our will and intellect to decide to forgive. It is not a feeling; we need to decide to forgive. Yet it is also a process because we have a right to work through the hurt with a safe person who is helpful and will validate our feelings, such as a priest, a therapist, or perhaps a spouse—if the offense is not against the spouse. Do not wait to feel like you need to forgive, because that may never happen.

That said, if you find it very difficult to forgive, the first place to start is with prayer: Ask God for the grace to decide to forgive as you process the hurts with someone you trust. Numerous psychological studies suggest that even the act of saying "I forgive you, [NAME]" can eventually lead to healing. We sometimes need to "act our way into being" in order to decide to forgive. But also recognize that we need to process the feelings of hurt with a safe person who will listen and help.

3rd Block: Forgiveness Does Not Excuse

Forgiving someone does not, in any way, excuse the hurt that was caused. Rather, forgiving is a decision to let go of retribution and to let God begin to heal and restore the relationship. When we let go of the hurt, God can start to redeem it and bring good from it. Jim witnessed this in a powerful way with a couple he was seeing for years to heal an addiction to pornography. The wife eventually forgave her husband, but she still needed to process the hurt and recognize that forgiving her husband did not excuse or minimize the sin. God did eventually bring good from this sin by using this couple as a means of healing other martial relationships similarly tormented by pornography.

4th Block: Forgiveness is Not Reconciliation

Forgiveness may be the first step toward reconciliation, but reconciliation is about wholeness and right relationship. In situations where the person has died, or if it is not possible to have true reconciliation, forgiveness is still a healing reality for the person who chooses to forgive. I have worked with many survivors of sexual abuse, and I seldom recommend that they reconcile with their abuser, which is usually not needed to heal. Forgiveness, however, is always needed in order to heal. In the case of marriage, we hope and pray that forgiveness will lead to reconciliation in the relationship. This may take time, but it is possible.

5th Block: Forgiveness Must be God-Centered

If we focus on ourselves too much, we may never decide to forgive. But if we focus on the healing power of God and invite God into this process, forgiveness is much more attainable. During the forgiveness process we may need to grieve over the hurt we experienced with someone we trust. That is good and healing. Remember that Christ cried when He grieved, and thus we can follow His lead. Tears can be healing. When we Christians do grief work we know that ultimately the Holy Spirit can transform the grief into gratitude. Jim will always remember a Catholic couple who was in counseling with him to heal an affair. They both continue to report that forgiveness has created a better marriage for them. The marriage will never be the same, Jim told them, but it can be so much better because God wants to bring new life from all our "death" experiences.

6th Block: Use Rituals to Forgive and Heal

Catholics understand that rituals speak truths that words cannot. Using rituals can help the healing go deeper into the soul and emotions instead of simply staying in the intellect. An example of such a ritual is to privately write down all your hurts and then safely burn the paper either alone or as a couple. If you choose to do this, watch the ritual. The ash is a different substance from the paper (a chemical change). And ash can be used as a fertilizer. A few hundred years ago ash was even used to make soap! This is exactly what God wants to do with our hurts as well. When we give our hurts to God, He will turn them into good. If we choose to hold onto our hurts, however, God respects our free will and may not be able to transform them into the new life He wants for us. We can offer God all our hurts during the Penitential Act (and at other times) of the Eucharist. Give them to God! Use a ritual act if you find it helpful.

7th Block: You Have a Right to Your Justified Anger

. . . but you do not have a right to take that anger out on yourself, your loved ones, or your spouse. A formula that can help is: contain, maintain, and re-train.

Think of an "anger safe" as a place to temporarily "contain" your anger. Never deny, suppress, or repress anger. In fact, when you are angry over an injustice, validate the feeling. How? Tell yourself that you have a right to your anger. Put all your daily anger in your "anger safe" and tell it that you will get to it later that day. In doing this, you "maintain" the mood you were in before the anger came and do not allow the anger to spread.

The last step is to "re-train" yourself to do something positive with anger before it does something negative with you. For example, set aside time to journal your anger out, think about the source of the anger, talk it out, exercise it out, pray it out, etc. If you exercise and start to sweat, that is when you can open your "anger safe" and let go of the anger. In this way, you harness the anger and control it so that it does not control you. We have both had cathartic cries on the treadmill as we exercise out our anger. As members of the Body of Christ we have dominion over anger and hurt, and by the power of the Holy Spirit we can do good things with it.

8th Block: Forgive and Forget ... Not!

We are not sure who coined the phrase "forgive and forget," but let's set the record straight: Only God is fully capable of that and, even then, God forgives and redeems. When it comes to understanding forgiveness, it is good to understand how God made us. Women have larger hippocampi than men do. The hippocampus is a structure in the brain that is responsible for many things, and one of them is memory. Women remember differently (think six-story screen, full-surround sound). Men remember in much less detail (think black-and-white stick figures). Jim has heard this from so many couples over the years:

Wife: "Jim, I just can't forget this thing he did."
Husband: "Jim, I can't even remember what she just can't forget."
Both reactions are appropriate and right! The next time you hear "forgive and forget," think about the differences between men and women as it relates to brain chemistry, because if it happens, it probably happens more with males than females.

9th Block: Understand the Power of Words

If you say to a co-worker or loved one, "I'm sorry about that," what will be the response 90% of the time? "It's OK." This is not a good formula for forgiveness because it invalidates the entire apology. It really *isn't* OK because someone was hurt. The next time someone apologizes to you, instead of saying "It's OK," say "I forgive you." Or, if you can't decide to forgive at that time, say, "Thank you for the apology." Then work through the hurt with a trusted person and decide later to forgive the person. The sooner we can audibly say the words "I forgive you, (fill in the person's name)," the sooner healing can happen, because we are meaning-makers through the power of the Holy Spirit. The words we speak are powerful!

10th Block: Learn to Forgive Yourself

Maureen taught this to Jim years ago. Jim had asked her to forgive him and she did. Then she looked at him and asked, "Do you forgive yourself?" He hadn't thought about that, but it sounded really good. He thought, "Why would I withhold something that Abba so freely gives to me through His Son, Jesus?" Since then he has made it a habit to forgive himself. After he asks God for forgiveness he likes to put his hand on his heart and say, "I forgive you, Jim." This has been a freeing ritual for him and for many others with whom he works, all thanks to the Lord, working through his wife Maureen.

11th Block: When the Offender Doesn't Say "I'm Sorry"

Again, work through the hurt and pray for the grace to forgive. The Lord will eventually give you the grace to decide to forgive even when the person doesn't apologize or ask for forgiveness (or cannot because of death or being out of reach, etc.). Forgive the person anyway, and it will help your physical, spiritual, emotional, and relational health.

12th Block: Conflict Redemption

There are literally dozens of books on conflict resolution, and you could probably find decent information by a Google search of "conflict resolution." However, you will find very little written on conflict redemption. While conflict resolution is a good and necessary first step towards harmony in a marriage, we believe that as Christians, Jesus invites us to do more. Here is what we mean.

Let's begin with some practices that assist in conflict resolution:

- Forgiveness must be present. We need to forgive before we implement conflict redemption.
- Never make your spouse the problem. Instead, learn the lesson of Jesus in the Gospel and make the problem the problem.
- When possible, learn how to "disagree with grace."
- If the same painful topic comes up over and over again, it could be an indicator that you need outside help (spiritual direction, therapy, coaching, etc.).
- Understand how your parents dealt with conflict and learn from it, trying not to repeat unhealthy patterns.
- Use "adult time-outs" to "cool off" and take care of your own anger issues.
- Use "safe phrases" when a conflict comes up. A safe phrase is agreed upon by both spouses when conflict is low and can be used in a marriage when conflict arises. It is similar to having a fire extinguisher in your kitchen. If a fire happened you would know what to do. Safe phrases can be used when there are "fires" in the marriage. An example of agreed upon safe phrases could be: "I need a different volume or tone right now." If that is agreed upon by both spouses, it can be used when there is a conflict. Once it is used, the offending spouse agrees upon apologizing and using a different tone or volume.

Once you have practiced some of these principles, it can be time to enter into conflict redemption. At the heart of this practice is the Catholic teaching that we all share in the priesthood of Jesus Christ—some as ordained priests, others as members of the "priesthood of the baptized." One of the key functions of a priest is to offer sacrifice and to "make holy" the things of this world.

In conflict redemption, we seek to "make holy" the very conflict that is drawing us apart. When there is conflict in a marriage, we need to work through it positively through conflict resolution. Once we have done that, both spouses can "lift up" that sacrifice of conflict to the Father as a sacred prayer. Doing this consistently serves as a knockout blow to Satan while healing our wounds because that which was used to work against us is now being used as a prayer in the Body of Christ! Memorize this passage: Romans 8:28 – it is essential for conflict redemption.

Reflection Questions on Building a Domestic Penitential Act

Answer the questions individually first and then share your responses with your spouse:

1. What role does the Sacrament of Reconciliation fill in your life? What role does it fill in your marriage?

_____

_____

_____

_____

_____

2. God desires that we seek forgiveness every day from God, others we have hurt, and even ourselves. Are there any areas (past or present) in your marriage that need forgiveness? If so, what is your plan to forgive these hurts and allow God to heal and restore?

_____

_____

_____

_____

_____

3. Does your marriage (and family) have and use a daily ritual of forgiveness? For example, at prayer time in our house we try to begin, as the liturgy does, with asking for forgiveness for anything that we need to. We as the parents start. If you do not have this ritual, does it appeal to you? How can you envision your family using it?

_____

_____

_____

_____

_____

4. What are the conflicts in your marriage that you need to first work through with conflict resolution?

_____

_____

_____

_____

_____

5. How can conflict redemption bring ultimate hope to these conflicts, as we have faith that "all things work for good for those who love God" (Rom. 8:28)?

_____

_____

_____

_____

_____

The Liturgy of the Word

4

After the Penitential Act, we pray the Gloria (if it is not Advent or Lent) and then move into the Liturgy of the Word. It is a profound encounter with our shared sacred history and is very active with many different types of intimacies, including:

- **Verbal intimacy** (we proclaim the living Word of God)

- **Spiritual intimacy** (we allow the Word of God to transform us)

- **Emotional intimacy** (we sing the psalm in response to God's immense love for us)

- **Family intimacy** (we listen attentively as sons and daughters of God)

- **Physical intimacy** (at the proclamation of the Gospel, we bless our foreheads, lips, and hearts with our thumb)

The Catholic Church has always "venerated the divine Scriptures as she venerates the Body of the Lord" (Dei Verbum, 21). This is a striking quote that many Catholics may not be familiar with. Here is another:

"Ignorance of Scripture is ignorance of Christ."

This pointed warning from the great Scripture scholar and translator St. Jerome summarizes the critical importance of loving, learning, and living the Word

The Liturgy of the Word is that time during the Eucharistic gathering when the community remembers its story in order to:

- Thank God for what He has done for us as a people.
- Come to new understandings of God's working in our history.
- Impart this memory to newer members of the community.
- Understand our current lives as part of the ongoing story.
- Search out the ways God is working to bring us to a future full of hope.

We enter more richly and deeply into the Liturgy of the Word by appreciating the historical context of the Scriptures as well as the ways the Spirit continues to speak to us through them today. This requires a few basic but important steps:

1. Regular time spent in prayer with Scripture.
2. An ongoing effort to learn about Scripture and the ways the Church uses it in the liturgy.
3. An understanding of both covenant history and "real presence."

This third point bears some explanation. Briefly, covenant history is a way of describing the overarching theme of the Bible. It is God seeking us out, revealing Himself to us, and saving us through His promises and ultimately, through His Son.

Rather than a neatly laid out explication of how God chose and saved His people, the Bible is a holy treasury of stories that carry out this plot, each in its unique setting, colored by its time, place, and author. For example, the mighty events in the Book of Exodus tell the story in quite a different way from the features in the Book of Jonah. But both speak of a God who is intimately involved in the lives of His people and who brings them forth from death to life.

Biblical covenant history, which is the main theme of the Bible, comes to fulfillment in the living Body and Blood of Christ at every Eucharist: "This is my body, which is given for you. Do this in memory of me . . . This cup is God's new covenant sealed with my blood, which is poured out for you" (Luke 22:19-20).

Along with an understanding of covenant history, Catholics do well to cultivate an appreciation for "real presence" in the Scripture, as well as in the Eucharist. Here is what we mean: We must be attentive and receptive to the story that is shared with us in the Liturgy of the Word. This requires undivided attention, freedom from distraction (particularly electronic devices), and patience, to name a few steps.

Although this sounds difficult, it is rewarding as well. Our attention to the real presence of God in the Scriptures fosters awareness of His presence in the rest of the liturgy as well. It may be a fair question to ask: how can we appreciate the true presence of Christ in the Eucharist when we aren't attentive to God's voice in the Scriptures?

How can this be done?

Applying these principles to marriage, let's consider covenant and real presence in the context of married life. For marriage is also a covenant, and it too, has a history.

First, consider the story that each spouse brings to the relationship. Think back to your own dating months and years and recall how your intimacy and trust grew as you shared more of your story with each other. It was a sacred sharing, opening you up to vulnerability, requiring that the other receive it with reverence and honor—even the difficult parts.

Next, reflect on the fact that the two of you have a shared story. It was sealed in the Spirit on your wedding day, and it includes all the ups and downs of married life: the new experiences, the bitter disappointments, the challenges, and the joys.

As with the Liturgy of the Word, in order for our marriage story to flourish and for us to flourish in it, we should:

* Thank God for what He has done for us as a couple.
* Come to new understandings of God's working in our history.
* Impart this memory to newer members of the community.
* Understand our current lives as part of the ongoing story.
* Search out the ways God is working to bring us to a future full of hope.

Connections to Your Marriage: The Liturgy of the Word

1. Exercise a deep appreciation for your spouse's story (as well as your own story) and with your shared story. Identify some special features of your story that require sensitivity, reverence, and patience.

2. Make time to really listen to the story as it is evolving in the life of your spouse. Here are some ways to facilitate communication: on date nights, over shared coffee, talking with each other in the car instead of listening to the radio, on occasional phone calls, texts, or emails during the day, etc. (See the section on "verbal intimacy.") Note how important your "real presence" to your spouse is here. He or she needs your undivided, patient attention.

3. Spend quality time as a family in order to ground your children in your story. Help them understand that they are part of the story and that God is always active in their lives.

4. Consider the practice of shared *lectio divina*, in which you set aside time as a couple to break open the Word. Note that the results of shared lectio are typically the fruits of the Spirit (Galatians 5:22-23): love, joy, peace, patience, kindness, generosity, faithfulness, gentleness, and self-control—from which every marriage can benefit.

5. Adopt a yearly practice (perhaps around the time of your wedding anniversary) of reviewing your story to see how God is at work. What goals have you achieved in your marriage? How has Christ become more central? What have you learned from failures and difficulties? How do you perceive God upholding the two of you? What is God's promise for your future?

6. Begin a weekly practice of sharing the Mass readings ahead of time and talk about any insights you gain from them as you heard them proclaimed at the Eucharist.

Reflection Questions on the Liturgy of the Word

For this section, we invite you and your spouse to answer the questions **together**. Because you are discussing your shared story, we find it most helpful for couples to answer these questions together.

1. Do you and your spouse devote time to reading the Word of God? If not, how might you incorporate this practice into your marriage?

_____

_____

_____

_____

_____

2. What happy memories of your early life do you cherish and return to? What happy memories of the early years in your relationship with your spouse do you cherish and return to?

_____

_____

_____

_____

_____

3. Why is it helpful—even necessary—to keep these memories alive?

_____

_____

_____

_____

_____

4. How has the Spirit brought you to new understandings of the difficult chapters of your story?

_____

_____

_____

_____

_____

The Homily

5

Following the proclamation of the Scriptures, we next receive the Homily. We encourage the assembly to pray that the Holy Spirit will inspire the homilist to say what needs to be said. Also, the assembly needs to pray for the people listening to the Homily so that the people gathered will hear what the Lord needs for them to hear.

A good Homily is about breaking open the Word of God (from the readings of the day) and creating a dynamic bridge between the Liturgy of the Word and the Liturgy of the Eucharist. Ideally, the Homily contains excellent verbal, intellectual, emotional, and spiritual intimacies, among others. A good Homily during the Mass is always Eucharistic. That is, it always suggests ways we can live out the Eucharist we celebrate.

Excellent Homilies are Eucharistic by creating a verbal bridge very close to the end of the Homily. That bridge summarizes the main theme from the readings (an example might be the Catholic responsibility to vote with a well-informed conscience) and then ends with a statement that invites us back to the Eucharist.

In the example above, that statement could be "And that is why we need to come to the Eucharist—so that we may pray for a well-informed conscience and be strengthened by the Bread of Life and the Chalice of Salvation to vote with wisdom." This type of verbal bridge at the end of a Homily offers the assembly a natural transition from the Liturgy of the Word to the Liturgy of the Eucharist.

A good Homily is never about the homilist—it is about the transformative power of the Eucharist and God's faithful love. No amusing stories about a trip to the grocery store are needed. If a homilist self-discloses, it should be in service to the main theme of the readings on which he is preaching.

A good Homily always invites the faithful to understand the central truth of the Eucharist: God's love wins; death, sin, and suffering do not win; God's love brings resurrection from death every time! A good Homily requires a prayerful openness to the Holy Spirit and frequent reading of good material in order to break open the living Word of God. It also requires prayer, excellent communication skills, time, reading, feedback from others, and reflection.

Connections to Your Marriage: The Homily

A good marriage requires the same elements as a good Homily: prayer, excellent communication skills, time, reading, feedback from others, and reflection.

Our marriages are called to daily break open the Word of God to a society that is often sleepy and unresponsive.

The Sacrament of Marriage, ideally, is *always* Eucharistic in that it stands as an icon of God's faithful, committed, passionate, and intimate love for all humanity. The Sacrament of Marriage is never just about the two spouses; rather, it is about the Holy Spirit creating a new identity: the "we" of the marriage. The Sacrament of Marriage requires daily work and prayer in order not to stagnate into mediocrity.

Practical Ways to "Break Open the Word" in Your Marriage Today

- Remind yourself and your spouse who you are as a child of God. It might help to place a note on the mirror that says "I am a child of God; treat me accordingly."
- Take some time each week for silent meditation. Just as a good Homily is followed by silence, so a healthy marriage contains opportunities for silence.
- Create daily family prayer time to read the Word of God and let it challenge you.
- Create time for the "we" of your marriage to grow. If the Sacrament of Marriage is about being an icon of God's love for all humanity, then in order to connect with your spouse you will need to set aside time each day for positive talk. This daily positive talk time is not for discussing paying the bills, figuring out how to get the kids to soccer, etc. It is about creating space so that the "we" of your marriage can continue to be transformed.
- If you have been blessed with children, make sure that you are "marriage-centered" and not "kid-centered." In order to be good parents you must resist the temptation to make your children the center of your lives, which is idolatry. Children will be central, but not the center.
- Because all of these suggestions take time, energy, and prayerful openness, you will need to closely guard your time. Therefore, take time to talk with your spouse and see how you can create daily and weekly rituals to help your marriage break open the Word.

Reflection Questions on the Homily

Answer the questions individually first and then share your responses with your spouse:

1. Recall a particularly insightful or inspiring Homily, recently or in the past. What feature(s) of this Homily made an impact on you?

_____

_____

_____

_____

_____

2. What are some challenges that you, as a listener, encounter during the Homily?

_____

_____

_____

_____

_____

3. What is the relationship between the Scripture that is proclaimed and the Homily that is preached?

_____

_____

_____

_____

_____

4. Which of the 6 suggestions for breaking open the Word impress you as helpful practices for your marriage?

_____

_____

_____

_____

_____

The Creed and the Prayers of the Faithful

6

After the Homily there is a period of sacred silence, and then we pray our Creed and the Prayers of the Faithful, which concludes the Liturgy of the Word. Then the Liturgy of the Eucharist, which is the second half of the Mass, begins.

In the Nicene Creed we profess what we believe. It is called the Nicene Creed because it was agreed upon in the city of Nicaea in about 325 A.D. It was formulated to unify what Christians believed.

How often do we think about these compelling words? It is a good and holy practice to study the words of this summation of what we profess to believe:

> "I believe in one God, the Father almighty, maker of heaven and earth, of all things visible and invisible. I believe in one Lord Jesus Christ, the Only Begotten Son of God, born of the Father before all ages. God from God, Light from Light, true God from true God, begotten, not made, consubstantial with the Father; through Him all things were made. For us men and for our salvation He came down from heaven, and by the Holy Spirit was incarnate of the Virgin Mary, and became man. For our sake He was crucified under Pontius Pilate, He suffered death and was buried, and rose again on the third day in accordance with the Scriptures. He ascended into Heaven and is seated at the right hand of the Father. He will come again in glory to judge the living and the dead and His Kingdom will have no end. I believe in the Holy Spirit, the Lord, the giver of life, who proceeds from the Father and the Son, who with the Father and the Son is adored and glorified, who has spoken through the prophets. I believe in one, holy, catholic, and apostolic Church. I confess one Baptism for the forgiveness of sins and I look forward to the resurrection of the dead and the life of the world to come. Amen."

Reflection Questions on the Creed

Devote 5–10 minutes tonight to read this Creed and talk about it. Here are some questions that might help your discussion:

1. What does it mean to believe in things invisible? Do you believe in angels and the communion of saints?

_____

_____

_____

_____

_____

2. Do you ask your patron saint to pray for you, your spouse, and your family?

_____

_____

_____

_____

_____

3. How might you ask your guardian angel to help strengthen your marriage?

_____

_____

_____

_____

_____

4. What does it mean to you that the Lord came down from Heaven, lived, died, rose again, and sent His Holy Spirit for you?

_____

_____

_____

_____

_____

5. What does it mean to you that Jesus will come again in glory? Can this be an ultimate horizon for us to really see how important something is during the day?

_____

_____

_____

_____

_____

6. What does it mean that Christ will judge the living and the dead?
How are we as Catholics invited to take stock of our actions and attitudes?

_____

_____

_____

_____

_____

7. What does it mean to you and your marriage that you believe in the Holy Spirit? Do you pray to the Holy Spirit? Do you ask the Holy Spirit to bear fruit in your marriage?

_____

_____

_____

_____

_____

8. What does it mean to "look forward to the resurrection of the dead"? Every moment we have on this earth is precious and is a gift meant to be lived out to the fullest. Do we think about our own mortality in healthy, holy ways? Saint Benedict, for example, encourages us to "keep death daily before our eyes," not in a morbid way but in a way that instructs us to make sure we are not taking each other for granted or wasting time.

_____

_____

_____

_____

_____

The Prayers of the Faithful

After the Creed, we begin the universal Prayers of the Faithful. The Prayers of the Faithful offer us the opportunity to pray for our needs and the needs of others. Prayer is essential in the Christian life, and it is critical in our marriages! We must make prayer time a priority in our marriage because it is the very air that we Christians breathe. Without shared prayer our relationship with our spouse will die.

What is prayer? There are many types of prayers. We use the acronym **"Practice"** to teach families the different forms of prayers. We benefit from thinking about and practicing these prayer forms in our marriage and family.

"Practice" the following forms of prayers:

P = Petition prayer is asking for something.

R = Repentance is to turn away from sin and turn to God.

A = Adoration is praise and worship; e.g. listening to Christian music, praying out loud, etc.

C = Contemplation is thinking about or reflecting on a word or phrase from Scripture. One example is to contemplate the all-powerful name of Jesus.

T = Thanksgiving. Thanking God for all He has done is essential. The word Eucharist means "thanksgiving." Ideally, our lives should be lives of thanksgiving!

I = Intercessory prayer, which is praying on behalf of someone else or interceding for them.

C = Communal prayer. We cannot be Christians apart from a community. God desires that we worship every week with the gathered community and keep the Sabbath holy.

E = Experiential is praying with your experiences of everyday life. As it is written in 1 Corinthians 10:31, "Well, whatever you do, whether you eat or drink, do it all for God's glory." This is the "holiness of the humdrum" and we need it in our marriages. So when you wash the dishes for the eighth time in one day, you have the opportunity to lift that up as prayer!

Unfortunately, many surveys and studies indicate that the majority of Christian married people do not pray together. The good news is that when married couples do devote time for common prayer, it is a very powerful way to build different forms of intimacy in the marriage.

Do you devote time in your marriage for prayer? If not, please make it a consistent practice, a habit. If you have a hard time praying together, please be gentle with yourself and start somewhere.

Perhaps the best place to start is with prayers you already know: the Hail Mary, the Our Father, the Glory Be, the Rosary, etc. Simply make the Sign of the Cross, maybe hold your spouse's hand, and start to pray a memorized prayer together. The key is to start somewhere, and to let God nurture the growth.

good Topic for MOT (marriage on tap)

Reflection Questions on the Prayers of the Faithful

Answer the questions individually first and then share your responses with your spouse:

1. Do you and your spouse make prayer a priority? If not, what are some obstacles or distractions?

_____

_____

_____

_____

_____

2. Of the eight forms of prayer listed on pages 52-53, what is your favorite form of prayer? Why?

_____

_____

_____

_____

_____

The Preparation of the Gifts

7

The Preparation of the Gifts begins the second part of the Mass, the Liturgy of the Eucharist. This is the time during the Eucharist when the assembly brings forward the gifts: humble gifts of bread and wine, as well as our financial offering for the Church. The bread and wine are placed on the altar, and the money is placed by the altar.

The Preparation of the Gifts and the offering of our financial resources is also full of various forms of intimacy:

- **Intellectual intimacy** (we need to decide to tithe and support the sacred mission of our Church)

- **Temporal intimacy** (at this point in the Eucharist we have spent about thirty minutes together . . . with no electronics!)

The assembly often does not notice much of this part of the Mass because most of us are singing while silent prayers are said over the offerings (the wine and bread). Just because they are said in silence, however, does not mean they are less important. In fact, these prayers that the presider says are profound and beautiful. They speak of the holy exchange through which Christ assumed our humanity so we could partake in His divinity.

Now *that's* communion! Jesus desires that we share in His sacred divinity at every Eucharist. Can you imagine how our marriages would flourish if we all focused on this central prayer over the offerings?

The Preparation of the Gifts is full of emotional intimacy (we are usually singing), spiritual intimacy (through the powerful prayers of the Church), temporal intimacy (at this point of the Mass we have been breathing the same air for about 30 minutes, with no electronics!), and verbal intimacy (from the beautiful exchange of prayers between the presider and the assembly), and more.

During the Preparation of Gifts we like to spiritually "place" on the paten our marriage hurts, our wounds of the day, week, year, or lifetime. We also take time to spiritually "pour" our family, loved ones, hopes, dreams, and goals all into the chalice. We do so during this time because the Lord desires that we give Him our worries and cares. In the Bible we read: "Leave all your worries with Him, because He cares for you" (1 Peter 5:7).

When we take time to leave our worries with Him on the altar, we can be assured that the Holy Spirit will bring new life from them. God desires to transform our everyday hurts and difficulties into a whole new reality of grace and peace for our life. Just as the bread and wine are transformed on the altar, so, too, will our pain, worries, and stress be transformed.

Connections to Your Marriage: The Preparation of the Gifts

Do you take time to leave all your worries and cares with God on the altar at every Mass? If not, make it a consistent practice to do so—especially during the Preparation of Gifts.

The Preparation of Gifts is when we offer our financial support to our parishes. Do you and your spouse tithe? Tithing is when we give at least 10% of our income back to God (5% to our local parish and 5% to other charitable organizations). If you do not tithe, please pray about beginning this time-honored practice. You can start with a smaller amount and work your way up to 10%.

When we make tithing a priority, God honors and blesses that decision abundantly. Everything that we have is a gift from God, and the Spirit desires that we share these gifts. When we do, God multiplies them abundantly!

Our parishes need more than just financial resources, however. Our parishes need many volunteers to run the ministries that the Holy Spirit makes happen through the people in our churches. Is it a priority in your marriage to consistently share your talents with your parish?

Reflection Questions on the Preparation of the Gifts

Answer the questions individually first and then share your responses with your spouse:

1. How can the act of placing all your concerns, stress, and worries on the altar serve your marriage?

_____

_____

_____

_____

_____

2. What gifts of time, talent, and treasure is the Lord inviting you to share with your local parish and other organizations?

_____

_____

_____

_____

_____

3. One of the prayers the presider prays at this part of the liturgy proclaims that we share in the Divinity of Christ, through Christ sharing in our humanity. How do you show your spouse that he/she shares in the Divinity of Christ? Do you really believe that your spouse shares in Christ's Divinity? Do you really believe that you share in the Divinity of Christ?

_____

_____

_____

_____

_____

The Eucharistic Prayer

8

This brings us to the high point of the Liturgy, the Eucharistic Prayer. The third edition of the *Roman Missal* has 10 official Eucharist Prayers, but the most common ones are simply named I, II, III, and IV. These prayers are very old. One of the Eucharistic Prayers dates back almost 1,800 years.

Some intimacies found in the Eucharistic Prayer include:

- **Spiritual intimacy** (we are especially connected spiritually during the ancient Eucharistic prayers)

- **Physical intimacy** (during the "Sign of Peace" we shake hands, hug, or kiss our loved ones)

When the Church prays, She teaches. One of the best ways to grow deeper in love with our faith is to examine and understand the profound words of the Eucharistic Prayers.

In order to obtain the complete text of these prayers, simply do an internet search for "text of Eucharistic Prayers" and follow the links. Or ask your pastor if you can use one of the missals in your Church. These texts are also included in the paperback missals available at church as well as in publications such as *Give Us This Day* and *Magnificat*.

During the Liturgy of the Eucharist we give supreme thanks, we acclaim God as Holy, Holy, Holy, and we pray for the Holy Spirit to come down upon the gifts of bread and wine and transform them (this is called "the epiclesis").

After the epiclesis, we hear the Institution Narrative and the consecration. The Institution Narrative is that part of the Gospels of Matthew, Mark, and Luke that contain the words of consecration: "This is my Body . . . this is my Blood." (The Gospel of John has no Institution Narrative but rather the Lord's washing of His disciples' feet.)

The Eucharistic Prayer continues with "anamnesis," which is a Greek word that means "to recall" or "to remember." Theologically, however, this is not simply remembering the way a calendar "remembers" what date it is. Rather, it is remembering so powerful that, through the Spirit, the past is made present. In every Eucharist we participate in the life, death, and resurrection of Christ our Lord! We also participate in Christ's sending us the love between Himself and the Father: the Holy Spirit.

All this because the Eucharist is trans-historical: It crosses all time boundaries and is not subject to time in the same way that we are.

The great Eucharistic Prayer continues with the theme of "oblation" and the unblemished sacrifice of Christ. "Oblation" is a Latin word that means "offering." In the Eucharist the Holy Spirit works through the priest and the assembly to offer up to God that which He has freely given to us: His only Son, Christ our Lord.

In the Eucharist we participate in the salvation that Christ gained for us through His life, death, resurrection, and sending of the Spirit. As we participate in this sacrifice, we, too, become more of who we are as members of the Body of Christ, which gives us grace to love God, neighbor, and self more and more each day.

The Eucharistic prayer ends with themes of intercessory prayer (praying for the needs of the whole church—on the earth as well as those who have gone ahead of us) and concludes with the doxology and the "Great Amen."

Doxology is a Greek word meaning "glory." Toward the end of the Eucharistic Prayer we give great glory to God and rightly give God "all glory and honor!"

The assembly resounds with a loud, affirming "Amen," which ideally is sung in jubilation to confirm the entire Eucharistic Prayer.

Responding in Unity: The Lord's Prayer and the Sign of Peace

On the night before He died for us, Jesus prayed that we would all be one, as He and the Father are one (John 17:21). As the Eucharistic prayer concludes, we respond in two ways to signify that unity for which Jesus prayed: we pray together the Lord's Prayer, and we extend to each other a Sign of Peace.

Each of these practices is deeply rooted in our faith heritage, and both have applications to marriage. In both, we are professing the unity that bonds us as members of Christ's Body, which we are about to receive. We focus on our communal identity ("Our Father," not "My Father") and partake in a gesture meant to include all (sharing peace even with those we may not know). The inclusive, self-giving, and communal nature of these two moments is at the heart of marriage in Christ.

We find it instructive that the presider will say the word "peace" four times in the forty seconds before we exchange the "Sign of Peace." Listen carefully for this the next time you participate in the Eucharist.

This invitation to share peace is critically important in our world and in our marriages. We need to be at peace with Christ and ourselves, so that we can be at peace with our spouse and with others.

In order to live this peace, we need to understand how to experience physical peace in our bodies. The ability to live peacefully stems from our body's complex nervous system (NS), which is on call twenty-four hours a day (almost like a parent!) through the brain, spinal cord, and other nerves.

The human nervous system is comprised of many parts. Here, we want to focus on three: the enteric, the sympathetic, and the parasympathetic. Stay with us here: this is important and *very* applicable to our marriages! Let's examine these three as they relate to living the peace that Christ desires for us personally, in our marriages, and in our world.

The **enteric nervous system** (ENS) starts with an "e." The word "eat" starts with an "e." Everything we put in our body immediately enters the enteric nervous system. The ENS is a complex web of neurons, which runs from the esophagus to the anus. It is a lengthy and important part of our temple! Our food directly impacts our mood. We never want our food to be "SAD," (the "standard American diet."). If we eat SAD we will be sad, and the joy of the Spirit will be hard to show (not impossible, but hard because of the high inflammation associated with this diet). A healthy alternative to the SAD is the Mediterranean diet, which nourished Jesus when He lived on this earth. Decades of research show what Jesus knew two thousand years ago: that eating primarily plant-based foods, such as fruits and vegetables, whole grains, legumes and nuts, consuming healthy fats such as olive oil, and using herbs and spices to flavor foods treats our body well by lowering inflammation and other negative body responses. Additionally, since the gut is currently understood as a "second brain," housing chemicals such as serotonin, it logically follows that treating our ENS well will yield positive results for our mood and our emotions.

The **sympathetic nervous system** (SNS) starts with an "s." The word "stress" starts with an "s." Not all stress is bad, of course; after all, diamonds are a product of stress (i.e. the stress of weight and compression). The SNS is not bad either. It is the reason we get out of bed. The reason for being alert and the ability to read this page right now are both functions of the SNS. But many Americans operate from the SNS too long and never give it a break. A steady stream of stimuli from various sources (news and social media, communications, even forms of entertainment) keeps us literally "wired." We find it hard to unplug and let down, leading to anxiety, depression, burn-out, substance abuse, and other maladies.

The Lord created the antidote to this situation, a counterpart for the SNS called the **parasympathetic nervous system (PSNS)**. This word starts with a "p," and the word "peace" starts with a "p." The PSNS is the "peaceful" side of our nervous system. Engaging the PSNS more often throughout the day gives the nervous system a chance to relax and revive.

One simple and highly effective way to engage the PSNS is through 5 x 5 breathing (five seconds in and five seconds out). Don't hold the breath and don't hyperventilate, just breathe in the Holy Spirit for five seconds and breathe out your worries for five seconds. It's simple, but it isn't easy! If you can't do 5 x 5, then start with 3 x 3, or 4 x 4. I invite people to build up to at least 10 minutes of 5 x 5 breathing twice a day. While you are breathing in focus on a "peace-place" in your life. Feel that peace-place, hear it, see it, and use all your senses to imagine you are in that peace-place. For us, that is the beach. So, when Jim does 5 x 5 breathing he imagines he is at the beach! It is a wonderful break in his day and activates his PSNS! Research affirms the benefits of this practice for our bodies.

Does twenty minutes sound like too big of a commitment? If so, consider how much unproductive screen time you have in your life. This can help reframe the time investment of twenty minutes for your entire body to relax.

The next time you feel stressed, try taking a nice deep breath and saying the prayer, "In Christ, I am peaceful." This can help calm the mind and the body and can even prevent a marriage argument before it starts! If you are angry at your spouse (or a child), first do some good 5 x 5 breathing—this can create peace in our lives and relationships—exactly what Christ prayed for at the Last Supper!

If you're like the average American and need more help balancing out your nervous system, we understand! We have been there. In fact, we wrote a workbook on this subject called *A New Day in Christ,* which addresses stress management and ways to lower stress in our lives and relationships. Visit **www.catholicfamilyresources.com** for more information.

Another highly beneficial way to be peaceful is through exercise, both cardiovascular and strength training. Engaging in regular physical activities has multiple benefits for both body and mind, since it increases oxygen intake, blood flow, muscle tone, serotonin levels, and overall functioning. Research is now showing that exercise is a near panacea. It can be hard to do, or hard to start, and if that's the case for you, learn from the Lord. Jim's experience of living and studying in Jerusalem gave him an appreciation for the fact that Jesus must have been in excellent shape! Daily, He walked up and down those hills of Israel and he didn't eat SAD (the "standard American diet"). This helped his body, and it can help yours as well. Walking can be a great way to start exercise. Couple it with prayer (a Rosary or other prayers as you are walking) and benefit both your body and your soul!

Reflection Questions on the Lord's Prayer

Answer the questions individually first and then share your responses with your spouse:

1. How has the Lord's Prayer taken on new meaning for you since you and your spouse married?

_____

_____

_____

_____

_____

2. How do you experience the presence of Christ in those gathered around you at the Eucharist?

_____

_____

_____

_____

_____

Reflection Questions on Living the Peace of Christ in Your Marriage

Answer the questions individually first and then share your responses with your spouse:

1. What are some effective ways you take care of your nervous system?

_____

_____

_____

_____

2. Are there any changes the Holy Spirit is calling you to implement in order to be a person of peace?

_____

_____

_____

3. How peaceful is your marriage?

_____

_____

_____

_____

4. What can you do to bring the peace of Christ into your marriage?

_____

_____

_____

The Liturgical Flow

The Eucharistic Prayer teaches us many lessons in our marriage. One lesson we want to highlight is the idea of liturgical flow.

In the Mass, an order and sacred structure are followed. We never just receive the Body and Blood of Christ without a natural building up to it. In other words, we don't partake in the depth of communion intimacy (eating of the Bread of Life and drinking from the cup of salvation) until we have respectfully celebrated the other parts of the entire Mass.

The Church teaches us a profound lesson with this structure. It is teaching us that there is a sacred order toward intimacy and that we need to respect that order. Married couples who understand and apply this lesson of sacred order thrive . . . and those who do not are at risk of early death.

As in the Eucharist, there is a natural and normal progression of intimacy in marriage. Just as we never receive the Body of Christ without first hearing the Word of God (reception of Holy Communion outside of Mass is a special circumstance; for example when one is in the hospital, etc.), the same is true in our marital intimacy. There is, ideally, a natural progression of intimacy that starts with what we call **"foundational intimacies."**

If spouses are not obeying this natural progression in their marriage, there will likely be major consequences in the marriage's sexual intimacy. Too many couples try to start with sexual intimacy without understanding that there are many types of intimacy that serve as a foundation upon which to properly build a healthy and holy sex life. But our society promotes only an emphasis on sexuality, which can lead to devastating wounds in the marriage.

When these "foundational intimacies" are met, and when we understand the lesson of the Eucharist (of a natural progression toward deeper intimacy), then our marriages will thrive.

Eight Foundational Intimacies

9

Over the years of presenting and reflecting on this material, we have identified at least eight foundational intimacies in the daily life of marriage. These foundational intimacies are like the reinforced concrete blocks of a building. The deeper they run, and the more of them you have while "building" your marriage, the stronger your Sacrament of Marriage becomes.

It is not coincidental that we have already seen all eight of these "building blocks of intimacy" in the different parts and rites of the Eucharist. When married couples learn ritual flow from the Eucharist, they will thrive!

These are the eight foundational intimacies, all of which we have seen in celebrating the Eucharist:

- **Spiritual**. Praying together, going to Church together, reading the Bible or devotional together, etc. We believe this to be the most important one because we are made in the image and likeness of God. Sometimes our experiences in the physical world can work against us and we forget that we have a spiritual soul created directly by God.

- **Verbal**. Talking, listening, and reassuring each other they are loved, respecting each other privately and personally, etc.

- **Emotional**. Validating feelings, sharing feelings, creating feelings of security, processing feelings, etc.

- **Intellectual**. Sharing ideas, honoring each other, understanding differences between intimacy and sex, understanding different needs for males and females, forgiving each other, etc.

- **Temporal**. Hanging out together as a couple and family with no agenda and no electronics, working out together, doing hobbies together, etc.

- **Family**. Sharing family time together with no electronics, sharing meal time with no electronics, working together, etc.

- **Physical**. Physical appearance, hand holding, kissing. This is *not* sexual intimacy.

- **Intimacy of absence**. Christ taught us about this during His ascension into Heaven. This form of intimacy points to the need for proactive and productive separate time alone in marriage. This is a tricky one and needs to be understood and acted on, and is not recommended for couples who have long absences from each other due to serving in the military or opposite work shifts, etc.

Note that sexual intimacy is not on the list of foundational intimacies. That is because the more foundational intimacies can be met in a natural day-to-day ritual progression in a marriage before sexual intimacy is shared, the better that sexual intimacy can be.

"Going Through the Motions"

Sometimes we show up for the Eucharist and we don't feel fed. These are the times when we trust in the ritual flow, the prayers of others, and the fact that we are still transformed even though we don't feel it.

We are not our feelings. Our feelings are very important, but they do not give us an identity. Our identity is secure in the Body of Christ: We are members of that Body, and we are daughters and sons of God; this is our great identity.

During the times in our lives when we don't feel transformed in the Eucharist, we trust that it is still happening, as long as we are not eating the Bread of Life to our own condemnation, as St. Paul warns us about in his letter to the Corinthians (1 Corinthians 11:29). We interpret St. Paul's warning about eating the Bread of Life to our condemnation to mean that we need to be well-disposed before we receive the Eucharist. We cannot be in mortal sin when we receive communion or we will "eat" to our own condemnation.

This same dynamic is true in our marriages. Sometimes we don't feel like we have a union, but we are still a living sacrament. Sometimes the forms of intimacy in our marriages won't immediately feed us, but as long as these don't create resentment in our spouse, these intimacies can make our marriage stronger.

For example, there are many times in a marriage when one spouse desires sexual intimacy and the other does not. If sexual intimacy won't create resentment in the marriage, then it can actually help strengthen the marital unity.

If, however, sexual intimacy creates some type of resentment in one of the spouses, that marriage could "eat" (i.e. have sexual intimacy) to their own condemnation, and that sexual intimacy, which was created to help the marriage grow stronger, can then serve only as a form of division.

Jim has seen this dynamic in the hundreds of married couples he has worked with, usually when the husband wants sexual intimacy but the wife does not. If that sexual intimacy creates resentment for the wife, Jim usually advises the couple to not have sex. Who determines this? The wife does!

That may not seem fair to the husband, but here is why the wife determines if sexual intimacy might work against the marriage. Women's sexual response is more about the process and not the end result (i.e. having an orgasm). Most healthy husbands don't need any foundational intimacies to have a good orgasm.

But most healthy wives need at least their top three or four foundational intimacies met before sexual intimacy can even begin to start feeling good—and even then there is no guarantee the wife will have an orgasm.

In other words, Jim tells husbands: "You need to give your wife at least good spiritual 'intercourse,' emotional 'intercourse,' and verbal 'intercourse' before she can begin to enjoy good sexual intercourse."

We need to be open and discuss what creates resentment so that healing can come, and that sometimes means a period of abstaining from sexual intimacy. This can be very difficult but is sometimes necessary so that a clearer focus on the foundational intimacies can bring healing.

If your marriage is in need of some sexual abstinence, it is usually best to start marriage counseling as well.

When we create time and space to understand and utilize the foundational intimacies in order to create a healthy, holy marriage, we can avoid resentment.

Here are two more very important points on foundational intimacies before we explore them in depth:

- **Foundation intimacies are not to be used as a "hoop" to jump through to get sex** ... "I'll do these foundational intimacies so I can have more sex." That is not the purpose of this material. The purpose is to learn from the beautiful flow of the Eucharist and to imitate that flow in our marriages. We build up to receiving the Body and Blood of Christ in the Eucharist, and we build up to receiving sexual intimacy in our marriage.

- **Beware of the negative sides of foundational intimacies**. Favorite foundational intimacies can work against the marriage if they are done in negative ways. For example, if verbal intimacy is really important (and it is to most women) then sarcasm, the silent treatment, yelling, harsh tones—all negative forms of verbal intimacies—work powerfully *against* the marriage. If this is going on consistently, the couple may need counseling.

So, how do we know which foundational intimacies are most important?

Understanding and Utilizing Foundational Intimacies

Foundational Intimacy Questionnaire

Directions: For each of the foundational intimacies, circle the number that best describes how important that form of intimacy is to you. A "10" is the highest and a "1" is the lowest. Then, fill in what action(s) you need from that form and what time is best for that action to happen. For example: If spiritual intimacy is really important to you, circle the "10." Then, if the Rosary is one of your favorite prayers, an action might be: "Pray the Rosary with me daily or weekly." Next, fill in what time is the best to pray the Rosary; you might write: "At 9:30 p.m. after the kids are in bed." Complete this questionnaire alone first and then share your answers with your spouse.

Spiritual (Praying together, going to Church together, reading the Bible or devotional together, etc. We believe this to be the most important one because we are all children of God.)

How important is this to you? 1 2 3 4 5 6 7 8 9 10

What action do you need from this form?

_____

_____

What is the best time for the above action?

_____

_____

Are there any negative forms of this type of intimacy in the marriage?

_____

_____

Verbal (Talking, listening, and reassuring each other they are loved, respecting each other privately and personally, etc.)

How important is this to you? 1 2 3 4 5 6 7 8 9 10

What action do you need from this form?

_____

_____

What is the best time for the above action?

_____

_____

Are there any negative forms of this type of intimacy in the marriage?

_____

_____

Emotional (Validating feelings, sharing feelings, creating feelings of security, processing feelings, etc.)

How important is this to you? 1 2 3 4 5 6 7 8 9 10

What action do you need from this form?

_____

_____

What is the best time for the above action?

_____

_____

Are there any negative forms of this type of intimacy in the marriage?

_____

_____

Intellectual (Sharing ideas, honoring each other, understanding differences between intimacy and sex, understanding different needs for males and females, forgiving each other, etc.)

How important is this to you? 1 2 3 4 5 6 7 8 9 10

What action do you need from this form?

_____

_____

What is the best time for the above action?

_____

_____

Are there any negative forms of this type of intimacy in the marriage?

_____

_____

Temporal (Hanging out together as a couple and family with no agenda and no electronics, working out together, doing hobbies together, etc.)

How important is this to you? 1 2 3 4 5 6 7 8 9 10

What action do you need from this form?

_____

_____

What is the best time for the above action?

_____

_____

Are there any negative forms of this type of intimacy in the marriage?

_____

_____

Family (Sharing family time together with no electronics, sharing meal time with no electronics, working together, etc.)

How important is this to you? 1 2 3 4 5 6 7 8 9 10

What action do you need from this form?

_____

_____

What is the best time for the above action?

_____

_____

Are there any negative forms of this type of intimacy in the marriage?

_____

_____

Physical (Physical appearance, hand holding, kissing. This is *not* sexual intimacy.)

How important is this to you? 1 2 3 4 5 6 7 8 9 10

What action do you need from this form?

_____

_____

What is the best time for the above action?

_____

_____

Are there any negative forms of this type of intimacy in the marriage?

_____

_____

Intimacy of Absence (Christ taught us about this during His ascension into Heaven. This form of intimacy points to the need for proactive and productive separate time alone in marriage. This is a tricky one and needs to be understood and acted on, and is not recommended for couples with long absences from each other in the military, opposite work shifts, etc.)

How important is this to you? 1 2 3 4 5 6 7 8 9 10

What action do you need from this form?

_____

_____

What is the best time for the above action?

_____

_____

Are there any negative forms of this type of intimacy in the marriage?

_____

_____

Now that you have identified which foundational intimacies are very important to you, as well as what action(s) need to be done and the best time to do them, it is good to examine some questions about the foundational intimacies.

Reflection Questions on the Foundational Intimacies

Answer the questions individually first and then share your responses with your spouse:

1. What foundational intimacy/intimacies are strong in your marriage?

_____

_____

_____

_____

_____

2. What areas need some work in your marriage? (Please see the next section on "Improving Foundational Intimacies.")

_____

_____

_____

_____

3. What are the most important forms of intimacy for you?

_____

_____

_____

_____

4. What are the most important forms of intimacy for your spouse?

_____

_____

_____

_____

_____

5. What are two behaviors that you can do today to help your spouse based on this questionnaire?

_____

_____

_____

_____

_____

6. Did you identify any areas of negative forms of intimacy? If so, what are they and what can done to stop these forms? It is very important that all forms of negative intimacy are corrected.

_____

_____

_____

_____

_____

Improving Foundational Intimacies

Below you will find practical ways to improve each foundational intimacy. If you need more work on a certain foundational intimacy, please look deeper into that subject.

Ways to Improve Spiritual Intimacy

We believe this is the most important form of intimacy because when we unite our love to the source of love (God), it strengthens our sacrament of marriage. Here are a few ways to start today:

- Make the Eucharist a priority in your marriage and hold hands at Mass while praying.

- Take daily prayer time together and alone a priority, realizing that as married couples we are called to be living icons of God's love for all humanity. If this is difficult to do, start with prayers that you already know and go from there. Any prayer is better than no prayer at all.

- Look for support. In her role as a wife and mother, Maureen depends upon the support of her spiritual director, as well as the good Christian friends she talks to. Likewise, Jim has an excellent spiritual director and an accountability brother as well.

- Pull out your marriage vows, memorize them, and use them as part of your prayer together. We do this sometimes when we are having a tiff: Realizing that God has blessed these vows can take the fuel out of any argument.

- Do you bless each other before you leave for work? Or before you go to bed? You can bless each other by placing your hand on the shoulder or head of your spouse and saying: "May God bless you with a great day," or any similar words.

- Perhaps pray about leading a "Eucharistic Marriage Group" in your parish by facilitating a group as each of the couples in the group works through this workbook together. This could be a great way to grow spiritually together.

- Consider Eucharistic Adoration together as a way to deepen your spiritual bond with each other.

Tips to Improve Verbal Intimacy

God has a priority of communicating His love to His people. We need to understand this gift and realize anew how essential it is in marriage. We also need to recognize that true communication is lived prayer (John 1:1).

> "Kind words bring life, but cruel words crush your spirit."
> (Proverbs 15:4). "In the beginning the Word already existed;
> the Word was with God, and the Word was God." (John 1:1)

- Use the "Positive Cycle of Communication:" The first step is to use "Prayerful Thought." Prayerful Thought is about recognizing that when we talk to our spouse—or anyone, for that matter—we are talking to Christ. Prayerfully thinking about the words before we start talking can help lessen arguments, disagreements, and negativity. After "Prayerful Thought", LISTEN and CLARIFY what the person said, and make sure you understand what the person meant. To understand what was said, you may want to say, "What I heard you say was _____." If that was correct, great. If not, clarify. Finally (only after you truly understand what your spouse was communicating), VALIDATE and respond appropriately (this may include a "fix" or a response such as, "I am sorry that is going on."). Positive communication is tough work. It takes practice to break old habits, so be patient with yourself and your spouse. Pray about and think about this cycle.

- Understand that what is heard is more important than what is said. We all have "filters" through which we hear things. Make sure to clarify by saying something like, "What I heard you say was _____."

- Try not to carry on a difficult conversation after 8 or 9 p.m. Our wills and intellect need to be fresh when we discuss difficult topics.

- Always aspire to total honesty as a policy. The more light you shed on an issue, the fewer shadows there are to confuse you. WARNING: With more difficult or painful issues, please seek the advice of a pastor or Christian counselor before sharing and being "brutally" honest.

- If a lot of anger is present, give your spouse room and space to safely and properly diffuse that anger before your discussion. Remember: Anger is not the problem; what we do with anger, however, can be problematic.

- Understand how your parent(s) communicated, argued, discussed things, played, worked, etc. Typically we will parent how we ourselves were parented—or the direct opposite (it is our "default" setting). The great joy of being an adult is that we can take the good from our family of origin and leave the bad. However, we can only do this if we have looked at, been honest about, and understood how our parents interacted and how they raised us.

Tips to Improve Emotional Intimacy

- Are you comfortable sharing your feelings? If not, how did this discomfort develop? We were all born very comfortable sharing our feelings (through different forms of cries), so when we don't share our feelings as adults it usually means that somebody taught us not to. It is a learned behavior. The good news is that it can be unlearned, slowly, and a person can learn how to share feelings again. Jesus shared His feelings in the Gospels. If it is good enough for our Lord, it is surely good enough for us.

- If you are not used to sharing feelings, start with a confident prayer to the Holy Spirit: "Holy Spirit, breathe into me the understanding that feelings are important. I thank You that You will help me to name my feelings and share them with my spouse."

- Pray about who taught you how to withhold your feelings. That person is not the problem, but not sharing feelings is a huge problem in a marriage. Even for high intellectuals, sharing feelings in a marriage is critical. Start with some basic questions: "What makes you feel happy?" "What makes you feel sad?" "What makes you feel angry?"

- Try pulling out some old pictures or an old movie that acts as a cathartic release (i.e., it brings feelings to the surface).

Tips to Improve Intellectual Intimacy

- If you are not used to sharing many ideas, start with a confident prayer to God: "Dear God, You are the source of wisdom. Thank You for helping me to know what I am thinking and to share those thoughts with my spouse."

- If this is hard for you, but easy for your spouse, find at least one subject that your spouse likes to talk about on an intellectual level. Research that topic, Google it, perhaps purchase a book on it. Jesus broke into our world 2,000 years ago, and we know He can send you the Holy Spirit so that you can "break into" your spouse's world.

Tips to Improve Temporal Intimacy (being together without electronics)

- Try to go on a monthly date if possible. Pen these dates on your calendars, line up a sitter if needed, and enjoy each other. Make them a priority. They don't have to cost a lot of money; in fact, they can be free. But these dates ought to be life-giving . . . no movies or sitting in front of the TV or computer.

- If "hanging out together" is difficult for you, perhaps learn from Jesus' teaching to Martha and Mary (Luke 10:42). In this profound story we read that Mary chose the better part, which was hanging out at the feet of Jesus, not doing "anything." We can get too caught up in productivity and neglect the healing power of real presence in our relationships. If this hard to do, ask the Holy Spirit to help you to understand and live this truth.

Tips to Improve Family Intimacy (being together without electronics)

- If you are blessed with children, keep the boundaries appropriate between the spouses and the children. Children should not be aware of any sexual or financial difficulties in the marriage. We believe sexual questions ought to be addressed early and often at the time the child asks them (in age-appropriate terms, within the context of the holiness of our sexuality). And certainly we need to teach our children sound Catholic principles of stewardship (tithing). But let kids be kids—problems in the marriage are between the spouses and need to be addressed by the spouses ASAP.

- Do you make sharing family meals together without electronics a priority? Research shows that sharing family meals as few as four times a week with no electronics can really help our children.

- Play board games, cards, dominoes; they're a great way to be together.

- Get outside as a family as much as possible! Kids (and adults) need fresh air, exercise, barefoot walks in grass, and catching fireflies on a summer evening.

Tips to Improve Physical Intimacy

- Begin by realizing that feeling no need for touch is a learned response. Babies are all born with an innate need for human touch (unless there are serious problems with the pregnancy, such as babies born to mothers addicted to alcohol or crack, etc.). Later on in life we may learn not to rely on touch as much because of what others say or do (e.g., if we have suffered physical or sexual abuse). God can heal all hurts and desires that married couples bond with each other via physical intimacy of holding hands, hugging, and kissing.

- If this is hard for you, please know that you are not the problem. Rather, the problem is what you learned. You can learn a new, healthier response and begin to appreciate touch again. Say a prayer to the Holy Spirit to guide you in this transformation, and stay close to the Eucharist because, through this miracle that we celebrate, this response in you can be healed.

- Make a habit of giving each other a hug and a kiss with an "I love you" when you say goodbye to each other at the beginning of the day and when you say hello to each other at the end of the day. If you need to, start out slowly, and give yourself grace.

Tips to Improve Intimacy of Absence: Positive, Proactive Time Alone

- Do you practice positive time apart in your marriage? We all need hobbies that we do both alone and as a couple. Examples include: martial arts, gardening, exercise, individual prayer time, scrap-booking, playing a musical instrument, a sporting interest, etc. After time apart, we come back refreshed and ready to serve our spouse and family. If this is not a need, that is OK. But for some people this is a huge need. If this is the only way you are being "intimate" in your marriage, however, there are major problems for which you need to seek the help of a therapist ASAP.

- A healthy "we" can only be formed by two healthy "I's." Thus, make time for yourself to pray and play both as individuals and as a couple so that the married "we" can grow stronger. The need for this may wax and wane over the years, so please pay attention to it.

- It is critical to realize that some vocations and careers do not need this type of intimacy (military families, those working away from home many days a week, etc.). In these difficult cases the couple should use technology (texting, phone calls, FaceTime or Skype) daily, when possible, to stay connected. These couples need much prayer and help from others in the Body of Christ.

The Communion Rite

10

Words fail us at this powerful rite. The all-powerful King of Kings, who was before all time, and who created the earth we walk on, desires to be held in the hands of—and be consumed by—the created human. This desire of physical intimacy reminds us of the Garden when our Creator walked with us in Eden. The Communion Rite is full of profound intimacies, including:

- **Physical intimacy** (we receive our Lord!)

- **Spiritual intimacy** (there is a profound exchange of persons as we receive our Lord in the Eucharist. He becomes part of us, and we become connected to Him and each other more profoundly.)

- **Emotional intimacy** (often people's response to receiving our Lord in Communion is to cry—they are so filled with joy and elation that the Lord of the universe desires to dwell among us)!

The One who made the Heavens, our final destination, gives to us on earth the bread of Heaven in order that we may faithfully continue our journey home. After this profound encounter, this holy exchange of persons (the Lord's becoming one with us and our becoming one with Him and each other), there could be no better response than sacred silence.

The members of the assembly quiet themselves and reflect upon the impossible: Our God desires to become one flesh with His people through the Eucharist.

Connections to Your Marriage: The Communion Rite

At the beginning of this chapter on the Communion Rite, we called the reception of the Eucharist a time when "God desires to become one flesh with His people through the Eucharist." This is a mind-boggling thought, but it is exactly what communion is.

The Word of God tells us that a husband and wife form one flesh, one body. In order to become one flesh in a holy, healthy manner, the best we can do as married couples is to make sure we are honoring the sacred flow of the foundational intimacies we have already discussed. Doing so can enhance our sexual intimacy.

This great gift of human sexuality is very much misunderstood in our sex-saturated world. Jim has seen many couples who rely on Hollywood for sex education, partly because their parents didn't teach them anything. We trust that through better marriage preparation, that can change.

Healthy and Holy Sexuality in Marriage

There are still plenty of misunderstandings, however, when it comes to sexuality in a marriage. In this section we will discuss practical ways to create a holy and healthy sex life. Shall we begin? Great!

A few beginning principles:

- God is the author of intimacy, and intimacy is different than intercourse.
- Understand your spouse's preferred Foundational Intimacies and try to create them.
- *Understand "Sex 101" and why men **need** to listen to women.*

"Sex 101" is what Jim teaches the married couples he works with who need it. Men have to listen to women because men do not know what feels good for women. There is a biological reason for this.

In some translations, Psalm 139 tells us that God knit us together in our mother's womb! When a baby is first formed in the womb, there is a similarity between boys and girls. Though the gender is determined at the moment of conception (XX for a girl, and XY for a boy), differentiation occurs while God is "knitting." For boys, this consists of a testosterone bath.

But before differentiation of the sexes happens, the clitoris and the penis are the same tissue. This is the "tissue issue" that all married couples need to understand. Because the penis and clitoris came from the same tissue, they have similar nerve endings. That is the reason that a caress may feel good to a wife one second only to be a direct turn-off the very next! It feels like a moving target, because it is sort of . . . a very small moving target.

This is compounded by the fact that sexual climax for men is mostly about internal penetration, whereas for women it is more about external stimulation through the foundational intimacies. This can get very confusing if husbands don't listen! So husbands, listen to your wives because you need them to tell you what feels good to them.

- *The need to know your own sexual response.* In general, a husband needs to take the initiative and provide good verbal, emotional, and spiritual "intercourse" (or other forms of foundational intimacies) in order to make sexual intercourse good for his wife.

In general, women may need to be more sexually available (but need to offer this from a place of strength and not of resentment or passive aggression) and men need to understand this. A wife can offer her husband a "gift" of sexual intercourse, knowing full well that it may not lead to an orgasm for her (of course, it might, but then again it might not). A husband needs to be OK with the "gift" of sexual intercourse and understand that it may not lead to an orgasm for his wife.

- *The need to identify your own privacy needs (time, space, location, etc.).* For example, many husbands with whom Jim works can have sexual intimacy while the children are awake. For many wives, however, this is a "no-can-do" situation, which husbands need to respect.

- *The need to acknowledge your comfort level with your own body and that of your spouse.* We also need to communicate before, during, and after intercourse—what is good, what feels good, etc. And we need to realize the profound vulnerability that is at the heart of sexual intercourse.

- *We believe God is honored when we adopt a prayerful (liturgical) attitude.* Let all we do (even sexual intercourse) flow from the Eucharist and back to the Eucharist. God sees all and delights in good marital sexual intercourse. If this is new to you, think about breaking down the walls of the "sacred/secular" divide and realize that your marital sexual activity is holy.

- *Begin sexual intimacy with familiar prayers.* Have you ever begun sexual intimacy with a prayer?

Here is a great prayer we love to teach couples to use before they have sexual intimacy:

> "Bless us, O Lord, and these Thy gifts, which we are about to receive,
> from Thy bounty, through Christ our Lord. Amen."
> (Perfect prayer before enjoying intercourse!)

Impediments and Supports to Sexual Intimacy

We need to recognize and act on impediments and supports to sexual intimacy.

Impediments (in no particular order)

- **Masturbation** (this is a tremendous impediment, especially for men). When the body has an orgasm, the brain is flooded with an abundance of feel-good chemicals that are very addicting. If one is suffering an addiction to masturbation or pornography, please seek out professional and pastoral help. Jim has seen the Holy Spirit bring healing, so please know there is great hope! One such place of hope is **www.reclaimsexualhealth.com**, a Catholic online recovery site that uses helpful, current brain research to help people overcome sexual addictions.

- **Contraception**. The Church teaches the nature of marriage as unitive (bringing the couple together) and procreative (creating new physical or emotional life). These two natures of marriage can never be separated. Contraception tries to separate and split the very nature of marriage.

- **Hygiene** (smoking, drinking, dietary habits). Curry, garlic, onions, and other flavorful foods can take hours (and sometimes days) to clear out of our system. Add to this the fact that women have a much better sense of smell than men do and you have a possible "one-two punch" that could knock out a woman's sex drive—all based on smell! So on a date night with Maureen, Jim will ask her if he can order onions with his steak. He hopes the answer is "no," even though he loves onions!

- **History of sterilization**. Jim has seen how this can really hurt a spouse's feelings deeply. If this is occurring in your marriage, please seek out counseling. God is a God of new beginnings. In one case, the man actually decided to reverse his vasectomy, and his wife was so happy with him that it increased their deep love and commitment for each other!

- **Fatigue or kids awake/needing attention** is a huge turn-off for most women, while most men don't care.

- **Past hurts and/or attitudes inherited from family of origin**. It is good to understand what your parents taught (or didn't teach) you about sexuality. If there is past abuse, please seek out good counseling. God desires to bring healing to any abuse, and Jim has seen the Holy Spirit bring healing to those who have suffered abuse.

- **Sex as a weapon**. Sex should never be used a weapon or a manipulative tactic that says, "I'll do these foundational intimacies so I can have more sex." That is not the purpose of this material. The purpose is to understand the natural flow that the Eucharist teaches us with no manipulation at all, only love.

- **Entertainment**. Much of the "entertainment" in our culture is poisonous to the soul of marriage. What we watch, read, and listen to informs and slowly transforms our opinions. One husband told Jim shortly after he was married: "Wow, sex sure is overrated, isn't it?" He said that because he had allowed Hollywood to be his sex-ed teacher. Even our commercials are over-sexualized. One of the best decisions we ever made was to cancel cable TV because of the trash that is aired. Is the Holy Spirit convicting you to examine what you watch or listen to? If so, act on it today. God will bless that decision abundantly.

- **"Hard" or "soft" pornography**. Pornography is never good for a marriage because it uses human beings as objects. Humans are never objects; we are subjects (sons and daughters of God) and have great dignity. We don't like the distinction between "hard" or "soft" porn because Jesus told us in the Gospel (Matthew 5:28) that if you look lustfully at a woman you have committed adultery (no action needed). The great news is that the Holy Spirit can come into our minds, bodies, and souls and change our attitudes toward sexuality and help us understand that God loves us and desires us to be free.

- **Mutual orgasm**. Society has a false expectation of the "mutual orgasm." This idea of the mutual "O" puts a lot of pressure on both women and men. Theologically and realistically, orgasm doesn't have to happen at the same time as long as the male's orgasm is inside his wife's vagina.

- A huge impediment is not naming and fulfilling a spouse's preferred foundational intimacies.

These are some of the common impediments to a holy, healthy sex life. If one or more of these impediments is at work in your marriage, please talk to a licensed therapist who works with Catholics because healing is possible. As a Catholic therapist and Catholic life-style marriage coach, Jim has seen it many times. God is a God of healing and desires to continue to heal and bring Christ's resurrection power into our sex life.

Supports to Sexual Intimacy

- **The nature of marriage: unitive and procreative**. This is a great support when we recognize how God truly created marriage and act upon that truth.

- **Natural Family Planning (NFP) is an awesome support!** This highly scientific method of understanding a woman's fertility cycle is an incredible blessing to couples across the world. Even non-Catholics use this because it never pollutes the female body, is all natural, works well for postponing or achieving pregnancy, and the divorce rate in NFP practicing couples is negligible compared to the rest of society. The reason the divorce rate is so low with NFP practicing couples is that it works in harmony with the true nature of marriage.

- **Purity in thought and deed**. In general men need to guard their eyes because the male visual cortex is highly attracted to curves. Thus, when a man views a woman he is attracted to, it is critically important that he say something such as: "God, she is Your daughter; I am not going to lust over her. God bless our marriage, and Lord Jesus give me strength to say no to lust." In the same way that men need to guard their vision, women need to guard their tongue because they are so very verbal! The sin of gossip wounds the Body of Christ.

- **Communication, communication, and more communication!** This is a crucial support in sexual intimacy. If you need to, re-read the tips on enhancing verbal intimacy.

- **Friendship with other Catholic couples** (this is so needed)! We need to be able to get together with a few other couples who share our values so that we don't feel so alone in our broken world. The sacrament of marriage is awesome. We need to be hope for others on the journey because our nation is no longer pro-marriage but pro-divorce.

- **Prayer and Scripture** (read the Song of Songs with your spouse. . . in bed . . . with a candle . . . naked!). Prayer is critically needed in marriage. Perhaps re-read ways to enhance spiritual intimacy.

- **Having a thorough knowledge of your body and your spouse's body** (what areas are sensitive in a good or bad way) is vital to a healthy and holy sex life. Jim recalls working with people who were not aware of the clitoris in the female body. This information deficit needs to be corrected by non-shameful conversations about the beauty of our human bodies.

- **Secret signs of affection and surprises** (if your spouse likes surprises). We love using secret signs of affection in our marriage as a playful and discreet way of sharing our love.

- **Catholic coaching or counseling**. A number of good therapists and marriage coaches who are trained are available to help couples either heal or grow. Jim loves to work as a marriage coach and help couples go from "good to great" or from "great to excellent!" If you want more information about Catholic marriage coaching please visit: **www.catholicfamilyresources.com** (Click on "Catholic Coaching").

- **Saint John Paul II's Theology of the Body (TOB)** is a great support to the goodness of human sexuality. Saint John Paul II delivered his *Theology of the Body* in some 129 lectures between September 1979 and November 1984. This is a tremendous blessing to marriage and life in the Church. We thank Christopher West, who has made TOB applicable to every person! Learn more about Christopher's work at **www.christopherwest.com**.

Reflection Questions on Enhancing Marital Sexual Intimacy

Answer the questions individually first and then share your responses with your spouse:

1. This is what I find intimate and helpful in our sex life:

_____

_____

_____

_____

2. Are there any impediments to your sexual intimacy with your spouse? If so, what are they and how did they originate?

_____

_____

_____

_____

_____

3. Have you discussed these impediments with your spouse? If not, please do so soon. Healing is possible if both of you want to work at it.

_____

_____

_____

_____

_____

4. Finish this sentence: "The best way for me to enjoy sexual intimacy with my spouse is to . . ."

_____

_____

_____

_____

_____

11

The Concluding Rite

A Church in our town has a sign posted near their driveway. As people exit the church parking lot their eyes are drawn to the sign, which says: "You are now entering the mission field."

For Catholics, the Concluding Rite (or the Rite of Sending Forth) functions in the same way as that sign. It reminds us why we came to church in the first place. We came so that we may be nourished by God's Word, by Christ's Body and Blood, and by the movement of the Holy Spirit in the gathered assembly and in the preaching of the presider. Having been thus nourished, we are renewed in strength to go forth and build the Kingdom of God.

All through this book, we have been reflecting on elements of the Mass that inform our lives as husband and wife. How, then, does this last aspect of the Mass enlighten our approach to the sacrament of marriage?

Consider this: Just as we Christians have a mission to build up the Kingdom through our lives, so also do we have a charge to do the same through our marriage. In other words, our marriage has a mission.

The starting point of that mission is contained in the consent we gave, at our wedding, to the three questions the presider asked:

- Have you come here freely and without reservation to give yourselves to each other in marriage?

- Will you love and honor each other as husband and wife for the rest of your lives?

- Will you accept children lovingly from God and bring them up according to the law of Christ and His Church?

Of course, for each couple, this mission will be fashioned by the unique features of their lives: their work, their children, their health, the challenges they face and the joys they share. It will be molded by their talents and passions, their relationships with others, their involvement in the life of their parish, and, above all, by their union with God.

The Rite of Dismissal charges the assembly to announce the Gospel by the way we live our lives, and to glorify the Lord in the process. These exhortations speak of mission. We are called to be evangelizers, sharers of the Good News. We are called to glorify the Lord by the way we live our lives and by the way we live our marriages.

Take a few moments now to consider the "mission" of your marriage. How does God send you out into the world to witness as a married couple?

Reflection Questions on the Concluding Rite

Answer the questions individually first and then share your responses with your spouse:

1. Revisit the three questions for consent from the Rite of Marriage (p. 91). Can you still answer "yes" to each of these? How has your consent deepened over the years?

_____

_____

_____

_____

_____

2. Considering the talents, challenges, work, responsibilities, and other characteristics of your family life, how would you describe your mission as a married couple? What message or truth do you have to share with our world?

_____

_____

_____

_____

_____

3. How does the Eucharist strengthen you to carry out your mission as a married couple?

_____

_____

_____

_____

_____

4. How can you share what you've learned through this workbook with other married couples?

_____

_____

_____

_____

_____

Perhaps you could serve as a facilitator for this workbook in your parish—serving as a mentor couple to a couple preparing for marriage—or become involved in World-wide Marriage Encounter, etc.

A Word of Thanks

It has been a deep honor to be a privileged guest in the life of your marriage. Thank you so much for taking the time to read and work through this workbook.

Our deepest, most sincere prayer is that the material offered here will help you fall deeper in love with the Eucharist and each other!

Because the Eucharist is the "source and summit" of our lives, we know that God can continue to heal and resurrect every marriage whose spouses seek healing and wholeness through the Eucharist.

Thank you so much. May God richly bless your marriage with the peace of the Spirit and the power of Christ. Amen.

—Jim and Maureen Otremba

About the Authors

Maureen and Jim Otremba have been married since 1995 and both have been part-time stay-at-home parents since 1999. They have three children on earth and seven in heaven. They are frequent presenters of retreats and workshops for couples, priests, deacons and their wives, and lay ministers around the U.S. They have written several articles for the U.S. Bishops' website and have appeared on EWTN TV.

Maureen holds a Master's in Theology from St. John's University (Collegeville, MN) with a concentration in Scripture. She has served in faith formation, marriage preparation, university administration and pastoral care, and taught high school in both Catholic and public schools for 10 years. She has written for *The St. Cloud Visitor* and is an adjunct instructor of Theology at the College of St. Benedict/St. John's University in Collegeville, MN.

Together, they have co-authored a Catholic, catechetical pre-marriage inventory called "Fully Engaged" (**www.getfullyengaged.com**). "Fully Engaged" teaches our Catholic truths to engaged couples through a catechetical workbook, trained facilitators, and Catholic inventory printouts. "Fully Engaged" contains a *Nihil Obstat* and *Imprimatur*, is translated into Spanish, and is used in many dioceses throughout the U.S.

Jim holds a Master of Divinity from St. John's University (Collegeville, MN) and a Master of Science in Applied Psychology from St. Cloud State University. He is finishing his Doctorate in Psychology. He is a Licensed Independent Clinical Social Worker in Minnesota and the owner of, and a therapist at, the Center for Family Counseling, Inc., a state licensed mental health clinic in St. Cloud, MN (**www.healinginchrist. com**). He is a regular guest on National Catholic Radio (Relevant Radio)

This duo brings their personal and professional teachings to thousands of Catholics each year throughout the U.S. through workshops, Catholic workbooks, and retreats. They are authors of several Catholic workbooks, which are available on **amazon.com**, or through their website: **www.catholicfamilyresources.com**.

May God bless you and your family!

Note: Here and on the following pages, you'll find an additional set of Reflection Questions that mirror those in the previous pages. We've done this so each spouse has his/her own set of reflection questions and space to write answers. Feel free to clip these from the book so you have the flexibility of one spouse using the workbook while the other uses this section.

Reflection Questions on Eucharistic Theology

Answer the questions individually first and then share your responses with your spouse:

1. What is your understanding of the Eucharist? How has this section affirmed or challenged that understanding?

_____

_____

_____

_____

_____

2. How does the Catholic doctrine of Christ being around the altar affect your celebration of the Eucharist?

_____

_____

_____

_____

3. What are some of the factors that make it difficult for you to recognize the intimacy of the Eucharist when you participate in Mass?

_____

_____

_____

_____

4. The Eucharist is now seen as a way to "strengthen our baptismal life." What is something that you can do this week to strengthen your own or your spouse's baptismal life?

_____

_____

_____

_____

_____

5. Did you gain any insights from the "blueprint of every Eucharist"?
If so, how can they help you fully celebrate at the next Eucharist you attend?

_____

_____

_____

_____

_____

Reflection Questions on Music

Answer the questions individually first and then share your responses with your spouse:

1. What are the songs that you have memorized? Take a few minutes to list some of the top 20 songs that you know by heart.

_____

_____

_____

_____

_____

2. This list of songs is impacting you at an unconscious level, whether you know it or not. These are your "go-to" songs. Do these songs build you and your marriage up or tear you down?

_____

_____

_____

_____

_____

3. How might Jesus respond to the lyrics of these songs?

_____

_____

_____

_____

_____

4. Is the Holy Spirit asking you to examine your choice of music in your life?

_____

_____

_____

_____

_____

5. Do you ever listen to Christian music?

_____

_____

_____

_____

Reflection Questions on Eucharistic Predictability and Possibility

Answer the questions individually first and then share your responses with your spouse:

1. Think about the last Eucharist that you celebrated. What were some predictable elements?

_____

_____

_____

_____

_____

2. Would you describe these as negative or positive? Why?

_____

_____

_____

_____

_____

3. Think about the last Eucharist that you celebrated. Name some "possibilities" (i.e. features that were new or different).

_____

_____

_____

_____

_____

4. Would you describe these as positive or negative? Why?

_____

_____

_____

_____

_____

5. Think about the next Eucharist you will celebrate. How will thinking and praying about a healthy tension between Eucharistic predictability and possibility help you to more fully and consciously participate?

_____

_____

_____

Reflection Questions on Marital Predictability and Possibility

Answer the questions individually first and then share your responses with your spouse:

1. In the Gathering Rite we recall that Christ re-creates us every day in God's image and likeness. There is great predictability in that truth. Identify three positive actions or attitudes that are predictable in your marriage or spouse. For example, "I can count on my spouse to take out the trash without asking."

_____

_____

_____

_____

2. Sometimes predictability can take on negative dimensions, and God's possibility for our marriage can be obscured, creating marital stagnation. Are there areas in your marriage where this is true? For example, "Every time I bring up a difficult subject my spouse clams up."

_____

_____

_____

_____

3. Given what you identified in the previous question, how can you invite God to bring life-giving possibility into those situations?

_____

_____

_____

_____

4. What are some insights from this chapter that you will apply to your marriage?

_____

_____

_____

_____

In conflict redemption, we seek to "make holy" the very conflict that is drawing us apart. When there is conflict in a marriage, we need to work through it positively through conflict resolution. Once we have done that, both spouses can "lift up" that sacrifice of conflict to the Father as a sacred prayer. Doing this consistently serves as a knockout blow to Satan while healing our wounds because that which was used to work against us is now being used as a prayer in the Body of Christ! Memorize this passage: Romans 8:28 – it is essential for conflict redemption.

Reflection Questions on Building a Domestic Penitential Act

Answer the questions individually first and then share your responses with your spouse:

1. What role does the Sacrament of Reconciliation fill in your life? What role does it fill in your marriage?

_____

_____

_____

_____

_____

2. God desires that we seek forgiveness every day from God, others we have hurt, and even ourselves. Are there any areas (past or present) in your marriage that need forgiveness? If so, what is your plan to forgive these hurts and allow God to heal and restore?

_____

_____

_____

_____

_____

3. Does your marriage (and family) have and use a daily ritual of forgiveness? For example, at prayer time in our house we try to begin, as the liturgy does, with asking for forgiveness for anything that we need to. We as the parents start. If you do not have this ritual, does it appeal to you? How can you envision your family using it?

_____

_____

_____

_____

_____

4. What are the conflicts in your marriage that you need to first work through with conflict resolution?

_____

_____

_____

_____

_____

5. How can conflict redemption bring ultimate hope to these conflicts, as we have faith that "all things work for good for those who love God" (Rom. 8:28)?

_____

_____

_____

_____

_____

Reflection Questions on the Liturgy of the Word

For this section, we invite you and your spouse to answer the questions **together.** Because you are discussing your shared story, we find it most helpful for couples to answer these questions together.

1. Do you and your spouse devote time to reading the Word of God? If not, how might you incorporate this practice into your marriage?

_____

_____

_____

_____

2. What happy memories of your early life do you cherish and return to? What happy memories of the early years in your relationship with your spouse do you cherish and return to?

_____

_____

_____

_____

3. Why is it helpful—even necessary—to keep these memories alive?

_____

_____

_____

_____

_____

4. How has the Spirit brought you to new understandings of the difficult chapters of your story?

_____

_____

_____

_____

_____

Reflection Questions on the Homily

Answer the questions individually first and then share your responses with your spouse:

1. Recall a particularly insightful or inspiring Homily, recently or in the past. What feature(s) of this Homily made an impact on you?

_____

_____

_____

_____

_____

2. What are some challenges that you, as a listener, encounter during the Homily?

_____

_____

_____

_____

3. What is the relationship between the Scripture that is proclaimed and the Homily that is preached?

_____

_____

_____

4. Which of the 6 suggestions for breaking open the Word impress you as helpful practices for your marriage?

_____

_____

_____

_____

Reflection Questions on the Creed

Devote 5–10 minutes tonight to read the Creed and talk about it. Here are some questions that might help your discussion:

1. What does it mean to believe in things invisible? Do you believe in angels and the communion of saints?

_____

_____

_____

_____

_____

2. Do you ask your patron saint to pray for you, your spouse, and your family?

_____

_____

_____

_____

_____

3. How might you ask your guardian angel to help strengthen your marriage?

_____

_____

_____

_____

_____

4. What does it mean to you that the Lord came down from Heaven, lived, died, rose again, and sent His Holy Spirit for you?

_____

_____

_____

_____

_____

5. What does it mean to you that Jesus will come again in glory? Can this be an ultimate horizon for us to really see how important something is during the day?

_____

_____

_____

_____

_____

6. What does it mean that Christ will judge the living and the dead?
How are we as Catholics invited to take stock of our actions and attitudes?

_____

_____

_____

_____

_____

7. What does it mean to you and your marriage that you believe in the Holy Spirit? Do you pray to the Holy Spirit? Do you ask the Holy Spirit to bear fruit in your marriage?

_____

_____

_____

_____

_____

8. What does it mean to "look forward to the resurrection of the dead"? Every moment we have on this earth is precious and is a gift meant to be lived out to the fullest. Do we think about our own mortality in healthy, holy ways? Saint Benedict, for example, encourages us to "keep death daily before our eyes," not in a morbid way but in a way that instructs us to make sure we are not taking each other for granted or wasting time.

_____

_____

_____

_____

_____

Reflection Questions on the Prayers of the Faithful

Answer the questions individually first and then share your responses with your spouse:

1. Do you and your spouse make prayer a priority? If not, what are some obstacles or distractions?

_____

_____

_____

_____

_____

2. Of the forms of prayer listed below, what's your favorite form of prayer? Why?

_____

_____

_____

_____

P = Petition prayer is asking for something

R = Repentance is to turn away from sin and turn to God.

A = Adoration is praise and worship; e.g. listening to Christian music, praying out loud, etc.

C = Contemplation is thinking about or reflecting on a word or phrase from Scripture. One example is to contemplate the all-powerful name of Jesus.

T = Thanksgiving. Thanking God for all He has done is essential. The word Eucharist means "thanksgiving." Ideally, our lives should be lives of thanksgiving!

I = Intercessory prayer, which is praying on behalf of someone else or interceding for them.

C = Communal prayer. We cannot be Christians apart from a community. God desires that we worship every week with the gathered community and keep the Sabbath holy.

E = Experiential is praying with your experiences of everyday life. As it is written in 1 Corinthians 10:31, "Well, whatever you do, whether you eat or drink, do it all for God's glory." This is the "holiness of the humdrum" and we need it in our marriages. So when you wash the dishes for the eighth time in one day, you have the opportunity to lift that up as prayer!

Reflection Questions on the Preparation of the Gifts

Answer the questions individually first and then share your responses with your spouse:

1. How can the act of placing all your concerns, stress, and worries on the altar serve your marriage?

_____

_____

_____

_____

_____

2. What gifts of time, talent, and treasure is the Lord inviting you to share with your local parish and other organizations?

_____

_____

_____

_____

_____

3. One of the prayers of the presider at this part of the liturgy reads: "By the mingling of this water and wine may we come to share in the Divinity of Christ. . . ." How do you show your spouse that he/she shares in the Divinity of Christ? Do you really believe that your spouse shares in Christ's Divinity? Do you really believe that you share in the Divinity of Christ?

_____

_____

_____

_____

_____

Reflection Questions on the Lord's Prayer

Answer the questions individually first and then share your responses with your spouse:

1. How has the Lord's Prayer taken on new meaning for you since you and your spouse married?

_____

_____

_____

_____

_____

2. How do you experience the presence of Christ in those gathered around you at the Eucharist?

_____

_____

_____

_____

_____

Reflection Questions on Living the Peace of Christ in Your Marriage

Answer the questions individually first and then share your responses with your spouse:

1. What are some effective ways you take care of your nervous system?

_____

_____

_____

_____

2. Are there any changes the Holy Spirit is calling you to implement in order to be a person of peace?

_____

_____

_____

3. How peaceful is your marriage?

_____

_____

_____

_____

4. What can you do to bring the peace of Christ into your marriage?

_____

_____

_____

Understanding and Utilizing Foundational Intimacies

Foundational Intimacy Questionnaire

Directions: For each of the foundational intimacies, circle the number that best describes how important that form of intimacy is to you. A "10" is the highest and a "1" is the lowest. Then, fill in what action (s) you need from that form and what time is best for that action to happen. For example: If spiritual intimacy is really important to you, circle the "10." Then, if the Rosary is one of your favorite prayers, an action might be: "Pray the Rosary with me daily or weekly." Next, fill in what time is the best to pray the Rosary; you might write: "At 9:30 p.m. after the kids are in bed." Complete this questionnaire alone first and then share your answers with your spouse.

Spiritual (Praying together, going to Church together, reading the Bible or devotional together, etc. We believe this to be the most important one because we are all children of God.)

How important is this to you?   1   2   3   4   5   6   7   8   9   10

What action do you need from this form?

_____

_____

What is the best time for the above action?

_____

_____

Are there any negative forms of this type of intimacy in the marriage?

_____

_____

Verbal (Talking and listening and reassuring each other they are loved, respecting each other privately and personally etc.)

How important is this to you? 1 2 3 4 5 6 7 8 9 10

What action do you need from this form?

_____

_____

What is the best time for the above action?

_____

_____

Are there any negative forms of this type of intimacy in the marriage?

_____

_____

Emotional (Validating feelings, sharing feelings, creating feelings of security, processing feelings, etc.)

How important is this to you? 1 2 3 4 5 6 7 8 9 10

What action do you need from this form?

_____

_____

What is the best time for the above action?

_____

_____

Are there any negative forms of this type of intimacy in the marriage?

_____

_____

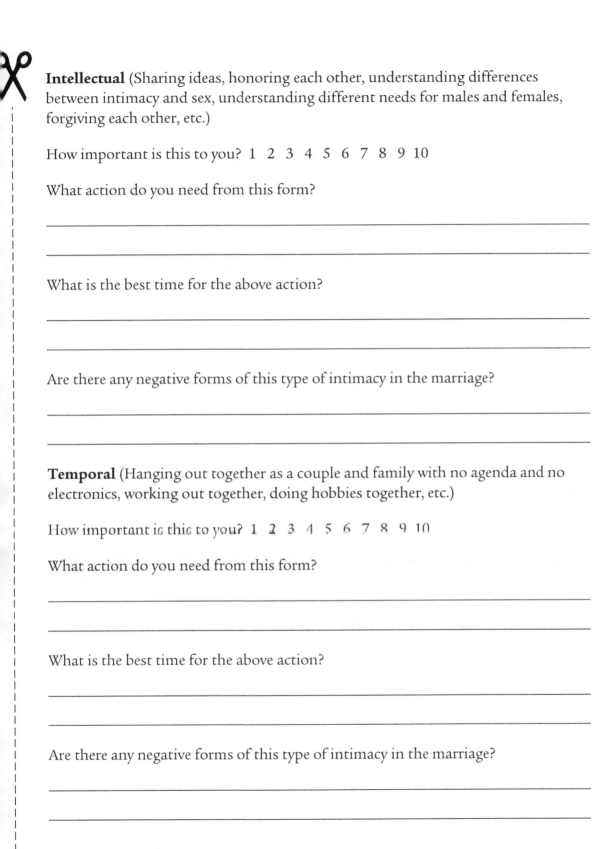

Intellectual (Sharing ideas, honoring each other, understanding differences between intimacy and sex, understanding different needs for males and females, forgiving each other, etc.)

How important is this to you?   1   2   3   4   5   6   7   8   9   10

What action do you need from this form?

_____

_____

What is the best time for the above action?

_____

_____

Are there any negative forms of this type of intimacy in the marriage?

_____

_____

Temporal (Hanging out together as a couple and family with no agenda and no electronics, working out together, doing hobbies together, etc.)

How important is this to you?   1   2   3   4   5   6   7   8   9   10

What action do you need from this form?

_____

_____

What is the best time for the above action?

_____

_____

Are there any negative forms of this type of intimacy in the marriage?

_____

_____

Family (Sharing family time together with no electronics, sharing meal time with no electronics, working together, etc.)

How important is this to you?   1   2   3   4   5   6   7   8   9   10

What action do you need from this form?

_____

_____

What is the best time for the above action?

_____

_____

Are there any negative forms of this type of intimacy in the marriage?

_____

_____

Physical (Physical appearance, hand holding, kissing. This is *not* sexual intimacy.)

How important is this to you?   1   2   3   4   5   6   7   8   9   10

What action do you need from this form?

_____

_____

What is the best time for the above action?

_____

_____

Are there any negative forms of this type of intimacy in the marriage?

_____

_____

Intimacy of Absence (Christ taught us about this during His ascension into Heaven. This form of intimacy points to the need for proactive and productive separate time alone in marriage. This is a tricky one and needs to be understood and acted on, and is not recommended for couples with long absences from each other in the military, opposite work shifts, etc.)

How important is this to you? 1 2 3 4 5 6 7 8 9 10

What action do you need from this form?

_____

_____

What is the best time for the above action?

_____

_____

Are there any negative forms of this type of intimacy in the marriage?

_____

_____

Now that you have identified which foundational intimacies are very important to you, as well as what action (s) need to be done and the best time to do them, it is good to examine some questions about the foundational intimacies.

Reflection Questions on the Foundational Intimacies

Answer the questions individually first and then share your responses with your spouse:

1. What foundational intimacy/intimacies are strong in your marriage?

_____

_____

_____

_____

_____

2. What areas need some work in your marriage?

_____

_____

_____

_____

_____

3. What are the most important forms of intimacy for you?

_____

_____

_____

_____

_____

4. What are the most important forms of intimacy for your spouse?

_____

_____

_____

_____

_____

5. What are two behaviors that you can do today to help your spouse based on this questionnaire?

_____

_____

_____

_____

_____

6. Did you identify any areas of negative forms of intimacy? If so, what are they and what can done to stop these forms? It is very important that all forms of negative intimacy are corrected.

_____

_____

_____

_____

_____

Reflection Questions on Enhancing Marital Sexual Intimacy

Answer the questions individually first and then share your responses with your spouse:

1. This is what I find intimate and helpful in our sex life:

_____

_____

_____

_____

2. Are there any impediments to your sexual intimacy with your spouse? If so, what are they and how did they originate?

_____

_____

_____

_____

3. Have you discussed these impediments with your spouse? If not, please do so soon. Healing is possible if both of you want to work at it.

_____

_____

_____

4. Finish this sentence: "The best way for me to enjoy sexual intimacy with my spouse is to . . ."

_____

_____

_____

_____

_____

The Rite of Dismissal charges the assembly to announce the Gospel by the way we live our lives, and to glorify the Lord in the process. These exhortations speak of mission. We are called to be evangelizers, sharers of the Good News. We are called to glorify the Lord by the way we live our lives and by the way we live our marriages.

Take a few moments now to consider the "mission" of your marriage. How does God send you out into the world to witness as a married couple?

Reflection Questions on the Concluding Rite

Answer the questions individually first and then share your responses with your spouse:

1. Revisit the three questions for consent from the Rite of Marriage (p. 91). Can you still answer "yes" to each of these? How has your consent deepened over the years?

_____

_____

_____

_____

_____

2. Considering the talents, challenges, work, responsibilities, and other characteristics of your family life, how would you describe your mission as a married couple? What message or truth do you have to share with our world?

_____

_____

_____

_____

_____

3. How does the Eucharist strengthen you to carry out your mission as a married couple?

_____

_____

_____

_____

_____

4. How can you share what you've learned through this workbook with other married couples?

_____

_____

_____

_____

_____

Perhaps you could serve as a facilitator for this workbook in your parish—serving as a mentor couple to a couple preparing for marriage—or become involved in World-wide Marriage Encounter, etc.

Made in the USA
Coppell, TX
12 February 2020